Beginner's Guide
to Coarse Fishing

Beginner's Guide
to Coarse Fishing

Arthur E. Hardy

with notes on tackle by
Alan Vare

PELHAM BOOKS

First published in Great Britain by
PELHAM BOOKS LTD
52 Bedford Square
London WC1B 3EF
DECEMBER, 1972

SECOND IMPRESSION DECEMBER, 1974
THIRD IMPRESSION OCTOBER, 1977

ISBN 0 7207 0585 1

Printed in Great Britain by
Galliard (Printers) Ltd, Great Yarmouth
and bound by Redwood Burn,
Trowbridge and Esher

Contents

Illustrations

LINE DRAWINGS

CREDITS

Plates 1, 17, 18 and 19, Dennis Gander; plates 2, 4, 5, 6, 7, 8, 11, 12, 13, and 14, Bill Keal; plate 3, Peter Grundel.

Introduction

Why 'coarse' fishing? There's really nothing very coarse about it. The roach angler, for example, uses finer lines and smaller hooks than many trout fishermen. The answer is that we use the word 'coarse' to separate the sport from 'game' fishing, which is the catching of trout, sea trout and salmon, and also from sea fishing. So this coarse fishing (we'll find a better word for it one day) really refers to the pursuit of a particular group of fishes, mostly belonging to the carp family, that inhabits the lakes, ponds, rivers, canals, streams, reservoirs and gravel pits of the British Isles.

Wherever you live in Britain, you're never far from a coarse fishing water of some sort, and even our big cities have canals or reservoirs nearby. Many waters contain a wide variety of species, while others are better known for their particular fish like carp and tench, or perch and pike. It is unusual to find water where just one species exists, except perhaps trout waters where coarse fish are kept out, intentionally.

To add to the general interest of coarse fishing, no two waters are exactly alike in size, shape, depth, weed growth and species of fish and, because of this, every fishery must be studied individually. As an example of this, I know two local waters, within seven miles of each other, both containing bream. One is a very shallow, weedy lake some six acres in extent; the other is a deep, almost weedless gravel pit of about three acres.

The shallow lake bream are extremely difficult to catch. They will bite very shyly around dawn and, occasionally, at late evening. During the daytime, they're almost impossible to catch. These fish will only take a maggot as hookbait and, when you land one, it's invariably a very light, silvery-green colour.

The gravel pit bream, on the other hand, bite right through the day, winter and summer, and will *never* take maggot; their favourite offerings are breadcrust and small worms. In general colouring, these fish are a deep olive brown, almost black on the shoulders.

Remember these wide variations between fisheries and fish characteristics when reading the general advice in this book. There are no 'hard-and-fast' rules in fishing, and all the baits and fishing methods we will be discussing are only meant as a basic guide. If this book can help you avoid the more obvious snags and frustrations that many beginners experience, it will have done its job.

Remember, too, that fishing should always be *fun*. A few hours away from the classroom, office or factory, breathing good fresh air and enjoying the delights of the countryside, will be so refreshing, you'll wonder why you didn't take up this really absorbing, worthwhile hobby years ago. As with most sports or hobbies, there is much to learn, but unlike many other pastimes, angling will never be *fully* mastered – and this is the beauty of it. However skilled you might become in the use of your tackle, however many large fish you might capture – even in very difficult circumstances – you will never ever know it *all*. Mysteries and countless challenges will remain.

Just to illustrate this point, a fortnight ago I fished a local tench lake and caught six, weighing over three pounds each, before noon. The weather was warm and windless, and I took all my fish from a favourite spot which I had 'groundbaited' the night before. A week or so later, I was there again, at the same place, which was well 'baited up', just like the first time. The air and water temperatures were checked and found to be almost identical to the week before. Using exactly the same bait and methods, I caught *nothing*. In fact, I didn't have a bite!

What's the answer? I don't know and, if I did, I'd probably

be there every week, pulling out fish after fish until I tired of it. But I have a feeling that, if this were to happen, my interest in fishing would decline, very rapidly.

When you first start fishing, don't be worried if you can't manage long, accurate casts right away, and don't be tempted to break the rod across your knees if you're not catching big fish the moment your bait hits the water. Take it all in easy, relaxed stages, and remember that things like learning to cast and mastering a fishing reel can be carried out on the garden lawn, or in a nearby park. But if you do practise in these places, please practise without hooks!

If you're going to take up coarse fishing seriously, you should obtain a book giving good colour pictures of all the species, plus notes on feeding habits, environment, breeding, etc. Get to know your fish – and understand them – for this will take a lot of the 'guesswork' out of your fishing. For example, as I write this, I have just returned from a carp fishing trip to a deep gravel pit in Essex. When we arrived, my friend and I saw no immediate signs of feeding fish, anywhere, so off he went for a thorough 'reccy' of the water. Ten minutes later he shouted for help, and I slipped the landing net under a lively seven-pound common carp. He had looked carefully at all the most likely spots, then decided that, if he were a carp, he'd be feeding in a particular part of the lake. As it happens, he was right. You see, he *thought* like a carp!

So take your fishing step by step, get to know your tackle and how it can be used to best advantage. With the aid of the 'Hints and Tips' chapter of this book, learn how to tie hooks, load a reel with line, and apply weight to a float to set it at the right depth in the water. Study, with great care, the various 'wrinkles' we have suggested, for they could well make the difference between a fishless day and a really memorable catch.

Try not to run before you can walk. Once you have a fair degree of skill in casting and general tackle handling, go after the smaller fish first, then graduate to larger ones. Roach are the ideal 'starters' and, fortunately, they're also the most widely spread freshwater fish in Britain, so you shouldn't have far to travel.

People take up fishing for a variety of reasons, but mostly as a relief from intensive study, work and family responsibilities, and all the other things that tax our well-being and sanity in this fast-moving, modern age. But of the three types of fishing, coarse fishing is, in my view, not only the most relaxing, but also the most interesting. To the average sea angler, strong seas, high winds and heavy rains are foes to be grappled with and beaten. He'll often swallow a gigantic fried breakfast at an unearthly hour, then take an impossibly small boat out in a raging gale, where he'll pump up huge cod or skate from the depths, using hooks the size of which would make a fine sensitive roach fisherman pale with terror. This tough, purple-faced individual is more mariner than angler: he eats and drinks far too much, and seldom speaks in words of more than one syllable.

Trout and salmon men can often be found, up to their wader-tops, in remote rivers and lakes, waving their fly or spinning rods for hours on end until wrists and arms ache so much that they are hardly able to drive home. They may sometimes be seen, after a day's fishing, regaining their strength with a glass of champagne or pink gin, in an exclusive club or three-star hotel.

Well, I'm sorry for that little outburst. You've probably guessed that it's no more than a good-natured 'dig' at our brothers of the angle who seek different pleasures. If the truth be known, I must confess to many an enjoyable day's fishing, spinning for bass from a secluded Irish beach, and fly-fishing for trout in a pretty West Country stream. And I have even been known to chase ferocious man-eating sharks off the Algarve in Portugal! However, my best love is, and will always be, coarse fishing.

This coarse fishing, well, it's really something else. To me it means many things. It can be fishing a weedy, shallow lake for tench, at the bewitching hour of dawn, when the rest of the community are still abed. Then there's the dreamy world of mellow eventide, just a half-hour before dark, when a good carp takes my floating bread bait – and not another soul in sight to help. I can remember crisp, frosty, mid-winter mornings in a boat moored off a reedy bay in a Norfolk Broad, watching my pike float riding the steely-grey wavelets, hoping for a fish, soon, needing the activity to warm stiffened fingers and hands, and thinking, perhaps, of lazy summer days on a fast, wide river or boiling weirpool, hunting elusive chub or big barbel, with only a herd of Jersey heifers for company. Yes, coarse fishing is all those things to me – and much, much more.

But for you, particularly at the beginning of your angling career, be a little careful of all this 'lone angler blending with the countryside' attitude. Personally, I usually prefer to fish with at least one companion, for, like all good experiences in life, fishing is much the better for sharing. In any case, when you finally graduate to the catching of larger fish, you'll find that two heads, and two pairs of hands, are often better than one.

While on the subject of company, you'll be well advised to join a good angling club, right from the start. You'll find most experienced coarse fishermen helpful, chummy types and, once they discover that you've just started the game, they will be only too pleased to give you advice on where and how to fish. If you're under sixteen, most clubs have their junior section, some even provide instruction sessions on tackle, casting, etc.

But whatever your age, the angling club could be your passport to a wealth of fishing knowledge and, just as important, will gain you access to the club waters which, in the main, will be well cared for and generously stocked with fish.

Private coarse fisheries are becoming more difficult to find every year, for obvious reasons. The rapidly increasing population means that more and more people are taking up the sport, so good waters are becoming scarcer – and more expensive. Exclusive specimen-hunting groups will take over choice waters, and pay very highly for the privilege. Nevertheless of all the various waters that I fish myself, the two most productive ones are both club fisheries – and one of them is even on a non-member's, 'day ticket' basis. So don't be dazzled by stories of fantastic private fishing; for, by joining a suitable club, you should find all the fishing you need, at least to begin with.

Besides, there are other considerations. Most clubs have their social side, so if you're not too much of a 'lone wolf', you'll make friends for life – and enjoy the company of people who have something very definite in common – a deeply rooted love of fishing.

Another good thing about fishing clubs is the almost complete breakdown of social barriers. I belong to one club that has among its members several tractor drivers, a few farmers, an accountant, two postmen, a Harley Street surgeon, three garage mechanics, six old-age pensioners, a freelance reporter, two representatives, a fireman and a millionaire property tycoon!

Welcome, anyhow, to coarse fishing. If the 'bug' should really take hold, as I'm sure it will, you're in for many years of joy, frustration, pleasure and bewilderment. In June, when the tench are on the feed, you'll be out of your bed before dawn, creeping from the darkened house in stockinged feet, to avoid waking the family. When August comes around, you'll make long, tiring journeys to far-off rivers, searching out the big chub and barbel. In the depths of winter you might even forsake television, hot roast luncheons and cosy armchairs for frozen feet, musty vacuum-flask tea – and pike. One thing you will discover: every single moment will be worthwhile, and one day, quite suddenly, it will all be made crystal clear. In the classroom, office or workshop, one of your colleagues will give you more than a casual glance, he'll regard you with a mixture of envy and frank admiration. 'Hey!' He'll say, 'You're looking great – have you been on holiday or something?'

You will smile, inwardly. But when it happens three times in the same day, you'll realise the truth; you'll *know* that you feel great, mentally and physically. Why, after all, shouldn't you? You've joined the élite – you're a coarse fisherman. Later in life – when non-fishing friends are jaded, grey shadows of their former selves – you, in your infinite good fortune will pity – and, perhaps, try to convert – them.

For you, having discovered the golden key to a world of

almost unlimited wonder and gentle excitement, will be scheming, in a wise and leisurely way, to find ways to increase your span of years; to retain your glowing youthfulness and vigour as long as possible; and to savour and enjoy each precious extra moment spent by the sparkling waterside.

CHAPTER I

Roach

Take an alphabetical list of rivers and still waters in the British Isles and you'll find very few that do not contain, or will not support, a head of roach. Equally at home in clear, fast-running rivers and in almost stagnant ponds, the roach is probably the most widespread and best-known of all our coarse fish; it's also the most obliging and convenient fish for the new angler to 'cut his teeth' on, as most roach waters contain large amounts of fish and they will usually bite well right through the year.

A roach of a pound in weight is a very good fish indeed, and on suitable light tackle it will give a reasonable fight for its size. A fish of two pounds is a specimen, and many experienced anglers fish for a lifetime without getting one of that 'magic' weight. If you catch a roach of three pounds, phone the *Angling Times* and they'll probably put you on the front page of the next issue! Just to whet your appetite a little further, it's known that roach of over four pounds actually exist.

But, as a beginner, don't set your sights too high. Concentrate on catching some smaller roach first and, before that, get to know why, where and how they can be caught. As a general guide, the smaller fish will usually shoal and feed fairly close to the surface, whereas the larger fish are less likely to swim around in big shoals but will be in ones, twos or threes, somewhere in the deeper parts of the lake or river.

Locating small to medium-sized roach, in a water where they're known to exist, is not difficult. Unlike some species of

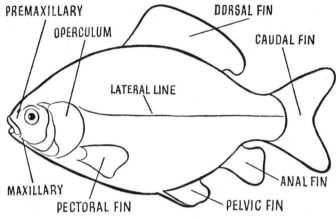

PREMAXILLARY

OPERCULUM

DORSAL FIN

CAUDAL FIN

LATERAL LINE

MAXILLARY

PECTORAL FIN

PELVIC FIN

ANAL FIN

The parts of a fish.

coarse fish, they don't favour any special feeding grounds, but will shoal, moving around the water all the time. The larger ones, however are a different kettle of fish, and will need to be located and fished for specifically. Every good roach water has its 'hot spots', and it will pay you to do some nosing around, or to chat with the local anglers, before you fish. In very fast-flowing rivers or streams like the Hampshire Avon, the upper reaches of the Great Ouse and on some Norfolk and north country waters, you'll be wise to find a slack eddy or backwater away from the main stream. I've had most of my larger roach from such places.

If you fish the big, well-known rivers, don't ignore the weir-pools simply because they look too rough or difficult for float fishing. The end of the pool furthest from the weir (which is called the 'tail') is a very good place for roach, but make sure that your tackle is not too fragile, for you might easily bump into a big chub or barbel there. Later in this chapter we'll deal with the actual methods of fishing, explaining, in detail, how to fish the fast and slow waters, and letting you know what type of tackle to use. But, sticking at present to the matter of *where* to fish, another good spot for roach is just to the side of a weirpool, where the water boils and froths like mad. It's usually quite deep there, and under all that turbulence, tucked away behind a big stone or bunch of trailing weed, will be a big roach or two. But be warned, and watch your step! Weirpools are nasty places to fall into.

Many city reservoirs hold big roach, and if you look up the record rod-caught roach lists, you'll find that most of them came from reservoirs, particularly those on the fringes of London. These huge, man-made waters require a rather specialised fishing technique, however, and to save a lot of heartache, I suggest that you give them a miss, at least until you have passed the beginner stage. Even very small farm ponds contain roach, and quite often they're the sort of waters that are ideal for the novice. The fish are plentiful and not too large, and most farmers will give permission to fish, if you ask in the right way.

BAITS AND GROUNDBAITS

Bread: in the hands of the keen roach angler, the humble white family loaf becomes almost magical! For general coarse fishing and the beginner in particular, it's clean, easily obtainable and much cheaper than many hook baits. In the special 'language' of coarse fishing, here are a few terms you ought to know concerning bread:

'Crust' is the outside of the loaf. Remember that even a small piece will swell in the water, so allow for this when choosing the size of bait. Always make sure the crust is well hooked to prevent it flying off when the tackle is cast out.

'Flake' is the inside of the loaf – the fluffy white layer just under the outer crust. This should always be as new and fresh as possible, and you should simply tear off small pieces to pinch onto the hook, but not too hard. Make sure that the hook point is exposed, as flake tends to harden in the water. Also, with the hook point at the ready, you'll be able to strike – and set the hook – much more efficiently.

'Paste' is made from the inside or 'crumb' of the loaf, preferably after it has gone fairly stale, but not sour or mildewed. The dry bread should be slightly wetted, then kneaded in a piece of clean white cloth until it becomes a soft dough. After a while, it can be kneaded in the hands and is ready when it stops adhering to your palms. Paste can be coloured or flavoured with various additives, but I suggest that you leave those little gimmicks until later, when you have mastered the basics of roach fishing.

Maggots: probably the most widely used bait for coarse fish, maggots are sometimes called 'gentles'. Most fishing tackle shops sell them, and they can be kept for quite a while in a refrigerator. The maggot concerned is the grub of a bluebottle, and after a while it will turn into a dark brown chrysalis – which also makes a good roach bait. Match fishermen use several other types of maggot, which they call 'casters', 'squats', 'gozzers' and 'pinkies', but I consider all this jargon to be a bit too technical for the beginner. In any case, you'll probably find, as I do, that the ordinary common maggot is as good as anything. Maggots can be coloured by the addition of harmless dyes to the sawdust in which they're kept, but although I have used coloured maggots on occasions, I'm sure that they haven't made any real difference to my roach catches.

An ideal container for maggots is a one or two-pint plastic 'bucket' fitted with a carry-handle and press-on lid pierced with air holes – but be sure the lid fits tightly. If maggots get out into the car or saddlebag, you'll be attacked by scores of angry bluebottles when they hatch out – I know, because it happened to me this summer!

Cheese: this can be a jolly good bait for roach – and some other coarse fish – but be careful with it, for it must be soft enough (just like bread paste) to allow the hook to pull through it easily when you strike. I can't stress this point too strongly, for like paste, cheese hardens in water, so make sure that it's pretty soft when it goes on the hook. The best type of cheese for roach is processed cheddar, which never gets really hard, but even this can be improved by the addition of some soft white bread – or white cottage cheese – to make up a nice soft paste. Other cheeses have been used for roaching, including the more smelly types like gorgonzola and stilton. It's up to you to experiment, but if you're camping as well as fishing, be sure to keep smelly cheese well packed up, or you're likely to have the tent invaded by rats and mice in the middle of the night!

Worms: not really the ideal roach bait, but on some waters, at certain times of the year, they will take the larger fish. The largest and most commonly-used type is the lobworm, which can be dug up in the garden or found lying on damp lawns at night. Brandling worms are a smaller type, and they have a curious ringed or striped body. They are to be found in compost heaps or under layers of rotting vegetation. Because of their smaller size and distinctive smell, they make a good bait for river roach, particularly when the water is flowing swiftly and coloured after heavy rain.

Stewed Wheat: in this convenient, packaging age, it is easy to obtain canned or bottled stewed wheat grains for fishing, and this nice clean bait is well worth a try. On some waters, the roach have been 'weaned' on wheat by the local anglers, and there are several rivers I know in Kent where this is easily the most effective bait of all. If you're going to prepare your own wheat grains, try doing them in a pressure cooker until they're soft enough for the hook – but not too soft for casting.

Hempseed: these little round grains can be bought in tins or jars ready to use on the hook, but if you prefer to prepare your own, get them from a seed merchant or tackle dealer, and boil them gently in a pot until the skin splits, and a little white shoot appears at the side of each grain. Don't over-boil them, or they'll be too soft for the hook. Some regard hempseed as a 'magic' bait for roach, and at one time it was even accused of being a drug to the fish, but this has since been proved untrue. Although I rarely fish with it now, I can remember some hectic hours fishing on the river Lea, when a few grains of hemp, scattered into the water, would bring dozens of roach flashing and swirling all over the swim. To hook a fish on hemp requires really fast striking. But, at times, roach of up to two pounds can be caught this way.

Other Natural Baits: besides maggots and worms, there are many other 'creepy-crawly' things to be found in the garden or by the waterside that, at times, will catch roach when all else fails. These baits include caddis grubs (the larvae of the caddis fly), beetles, live flies of all kinds, caterpillars, leeches, slugs, grasshoppers, spiders, etc.

Some fruits have also caught good roach, and elderberries (particularly where they grow by the waterside), bits of apple, pineapple, coconut, etc., are all worth a try when the roach are tired of the more usual baits. After all, if you had just finished a good meal, you could probably still be tempted by a bowl of chocolate mints, or a slice of exotic cream gateau, so don't be afraid to experiment with new baits, all the time. You might come across a real winner!

One very good natural bait for fishing weirpools is silkweed. This fine green weed grows on the 'sills' of weirs, and you should draw your hook through the weed, producing a trail about two inches long. Fished on float tackle, near to the side of the weir, this bait can account for specimen roach.

Groundbaits: groundbait is the stuff that you throw into the water you're going to fish, to attract the fish to your hookbait. In my experience, roach don't need heavy groundbaiting, and a few handfuls of mashed bread, or mixed bread, bran and sausage rusk, thrown in every few minutes, should keep the fish in your patch. In fast rivers your groundbait needs to be heavier than the type used in still waters. Most deepish rivers have a top layer of fairly fast-moving water, with slower, or almost static water on the river bed. To get through this top layer, the groundbait should be made up into gooey lumps about the size of a cricket ball, with a few small pebbles in the middle to help it down. Make up river groundbait with the minimum of water; you can even use some thick heavy mud to help bind it together. When using maggots as hookbait, put some in the groundbait; a few loose maggots can also be thrown in the swim from time to time to keep the roach interested, but if you're on a very fast-flowing water, remember to deposit them well upstream of where you're fishing.

If you're after the smaller 'shoal' roach, a good 'cloud' groundbait will help to attract the fish at about midwater. This groundbait can be made with fine white breadcrumbs, mixed with some condensed (not evaporated) milk to form a nice milky cloud or 'bomb burst' in the water. This really works – try it sometime!

Freshness: all the baits and groundbaits described should be used absolutely fresh. Bread, paste and cheese, in particular, go sour very quickly, and this tends to put the fish off; I suppose they have a built-in warning that tells them that mildew is not the healthiest of diets! However, one groundbait that will stand the test of time is the hard, 'open-end' type of manufactured blocks available from tackle shops. This stuff allows extra weight for long casting and, being hollow inside, can be filled with maggots (or other hookbaits), sealed up with soft groundbait, and left to settle on the bottom, giving a nice trickle of morsels as the inside titbits escape and the block itself slowly breaks up in the current.

TACKLE

The basic equipment for catching roach is pretty much the same as that used for many other species of coarse fish. Consequently, your choice of roach tackle is an extremely important one. And, because of this, I'm going to describe roach tackle in some detail.

When you go to buy your first rod and reel, take an experienced angler with you, if at all possible, to advise you on the right selection – but be careful whom you take! Remember that such a vital task should not be lightly entrusted to good old uncle Bert who used to fish thirty years ago when he was a lad, and not since. And make sure that you go to a good tackle shop, preferably one that specialises in fishing tackle, not the local pet shop or hardware store that sells a bit of fishing gear as a sideline.

The specialist tackle man is your guide and he will almost certainly be a keen angler himself – and 'in the know' on the very latest equipment. Above all, bear in mind that fishing tackle must be practical, and try to avoid the shiny, brightly-coloured goods that are on display in many tackle shops.

Although this stuff is most attractive, it's really designed to catch *anglers* rather than fish!

Rods: in my opinion, the best roach rod for a beginner will be a 12 ft to 13 ft match rod of hollow glass fibre. This material is light and strong, and it stands up to a lot of harsh treatment. Let's take a closer look at this rod. The handle is made from cork to give a pleasant non-slip grip; there are two 'winch' fittings on the handle, sliding metal rings that hold the reel firmly on the rod. These fittings must be a snug fit on the handle, so that the reel, once it is fitted, will not slip off in use. From the reel, the line will run up through the rod-rings, which are spaced along the length of the rod, and they get closer together as they reach the top ring.

On a match rod, the rings are made to carry the line well away from the rod itself, and they are called 'stand off' rings for this reason. The rod is usually in three pieces, or joints, and these are fitted together by means of brass tubes or ferrules. The best fibre-glass rods, however, are 'ferruleless'. That is, they have no metal ferrules, and the self-tubed fibreglass joints fit snugly into each other. When you're looking at and trying a new rod, make sure that the joints fit properly – that is, not too tight, nor so loose that they rattle when the rod is made up. Take a good look at the rod-rings, too. These should always be dead in line with each other, and the 'whippings' holding them to the rod should be well varnished to keep out weather and moisture.

Two of the rings should be lined with a glass-like material to prevent excess wear from the line. These are the top ring (at the thinnest end of the rod) and the 'butt' ring (the one nearest the reel and handle). Although these liners are very tough, they're also brittle, and they will become cracked through misuse. You can ensure that yours are in perfect condition by putting your little fingernail into each liner and rotating it slowly, for any small crack or defect will be felt at once, as it grates on your nail. This is a very important point to look for.

Having decided that your rod is well made, have a good look at its 'action' before you finally decide to buy. For general match fishing you should choose a stiffish rod that will bend down into the middle and butt joints when the tip is held and a firm, smooth, upward pressure applied to the handle.

So, the rod should be well constructed, the ferrules (or joints) should fit well, the rings be well spaced and in good condition. It should be light to hold, well-balanced and have a good action in the hand.

The last thing to look for is a good rod bag. This should be made from a strong material, and fitted with three compartments (for three-joint rods). It is essential that each joint is well separated in transit, as loose joints rubbing together can cause damage to the rings, even the rod itself.

Now you have a good 12 ft or 13 ft match rod, which should be ideal for all types of roach fishing, and other forms of coarse fishing besides. This rod will almost certainly be used for general float fishing, so let's now discuss some other rods that the roach angler might need to fish by other methods, and rods which can also be used to catch other types of fish.

Legering is a form of fishing that requires the bait to be cast out to a reasonable distance, then the rod is placed in a rod-rest and a 'bite indicator' is attached to the line, near the reel. With this method, a float is not used to indicate bites. For ideal legering, I would choose a rod of about 7 ft to 8 ft long, and again made of hollow fibre-glass, either 'ferruleless', brass ferruled or 'spigotted' – which means that it has an internal ferrule, a dowel-like projection from the butt joint that fits *inside* the top joint.

The rings on a leger rod are different to those on a typical match rod. They are closer to the rod, and are called 'full open bridge' rings. Also, the tip ring should be threaded to take a 'swing tip' or 'quiver tip', which are forms of bite indicator and will be discussed later in this chapter. The action of a good leger rod should be 'full' – which means that it should bend right down to the handle. Some leger rods are also fitted with 'screw winch' fittings, which have a threaded locking device for holding the reel on securely.

'Spinning' is a method of fishing for pike, perch and other

predatory fish, and many leger rods are ideal for this purpose. But, since spinning is not generally a roach fishing method, it will be explained more fully elsewhere in this book.

A third rod that could be extremely useful to the roach angler is the 'trotting' rod, which is mainly used for float fishing in fast-flowing waters, using a method where the float and end tackle follow the current downstream, with the bait 'trotting' or just tripping over the bottom of the river. The ideal rod for this purpose will be about 10 ft or 11 ft long, in two sections, and, preferably, very 'easy' in action. That is, it will be light and very pliable, right down the rod. Again, hollow fibreglass is the material to look for, a material that I have recommended for all three rods, as I believe it to be the finest available at the time of writing.

Other rods can be obtained made from 'split cane', which is also a good material, with a good action, but without the lightness and general durability of fibreglass. If you should be lucky enough to inherit one of these rods, or have one given to you, by all means use it, first making note of the general requirements mentioned under 'Tackle'.

Some leger and spinning rods are made from solid fibreglass, and these are extremely tough, almost indestructible, in fact, and they cost less than hollow types. But, quite naturally, they are much heavier in the hand.

Care of Rods: always take great care of fishing rods, if you don't, they're quite likely to let you down at the wrong moment – just like any other piece of equipment. I'll be dealing with rod care in greater detail, later in the book.

Reels: having purchased your rod, or rods, the next most important item is a reel. Of these are two main types, the first and most important to the beginner is the 'fixed spool' or 'threadline' reel. This type has the spool facing up and parallel to the rod, with the line controlled by a wire 'bale arm' and the reel handle geared so that one turn of the handle puts three or more turns of line onto the spool. For casting, the bale arm is opened so that the line may leave the spool freely. Line tension is controlled by an adjustment called a 'slipping clutch', which

25

allows line to leave the reel when the fish pulls its hardest, so avoiding a breakage. Another useful device on this reel is a 'non-reverse' lever, which prevents line running out from the reel when the rod is lying in its rod-rests.

There are many different makes and models of fixed spool reel, including some very cheap but attractively finished ones. My advice is to avoid those and go for a reel made by a well-known manufacturer – and always choose the best you can afford. Most good fixed spool reels come with two separate detachable spools, to allow quick switching from one line strength to another; for example, the smaller spool might hold 100 yards of 4 lb. breaking strain line, and the larger one about 200 yards of 9 lb.

There is another type of coarse fishing reel known as the 'centre pin' reel. This is a plain drum reel, with the spindle at right angles to the rod; it runs freely on fine bearings and has a pair of handles at the side, also a ratchet device to prevent the drum revolving too freely, when required. Its main feature is the ability to revolve easily at low speeds, allowing line to leave the spool without jerk or friction. This reel is a natural companion to the trotting rod already described, and can also be used for more general coarse fishing when long casting distances are not important.

I will mention a third reel in passing, the 'closed face' type. This is similar to the fixed spool ir many respects, except that it has, instead of a bale arm, a line control device inside the cover of the spool. It is the cover that gives the reel its name. This particular reel is often used in casting competitions.

Lines: having decided on a suitable reel, we must now buy some line for roach fishing. For general float fishing, we will probably use a line of about 2 lb. breaking strain and for legering and trotting one of roughly 4 lb. Legering and trotting are 'heavier' types of fishing, consequently, the 4 lb. line will stand the strain better than the 2 lb.

Here again, there's a bewilderingly wide choice for the beginner, so let's look at the problem in detail. Most anglers today use monofilament line – a single-strand line which will almost certainly be made of nylon. Make sure that you buy a well-known brand of line – and be sure that it is 'fresh', and not last year's, for example. Don't be tempted to get cheap line and don't waste money on the very expensive types; something in between is the best for the beginner.

When the tackle dealer hands you the spool, just feel the first few feet of line with your fingertips. Is it smooth and without lumps and bumps? If it is, then settle for it, it's more than likely quite a reasonable line. But stand your ground – we know you're new to the game, but don't be afraid to reject any line that feels like miniature barbed wire!

Any line is only as good as its weakest point, and assuming we have selected a line that's good and smooth, the weakest point on the line, when the tackle is made up, will be at the knot, or knots. Special knots are necessary for nylon mono-filament (see diagrams on page 109). Learn these knots well, by continual practice, until they are thoroughly mastered; your whole future success or failure rate could depend on it.

Floats: Now we come to one of fishing's most fascinating subjects – floats. There's such a wealth of good, attractive looking floats available that most anglers, even some very famous ones, buy far more than they really need. One or two of my own customers can't resist buying a new float or two whenever they come to the shop; I sometimes think they must have cupboards full of them at home!

So, to avoid confusion, I'm going to recommend a short list of suitable floats for you to start with. Firstly, there are the bird quills, these are usually strong, useful and robust floats, and in my experience, the best of the bunch is the peacock quill. This comes from the main stem of the long tail feather of the adult peacock and is often fully 3 ft long, with a slow taper to the point. It can easily be cut up into pieces of varying length and is ideal for roach fishing, particularly in still water.

Crow quills are a smaller, lighter type of float, and are normally about 4 in. to 6 in. long, slightly curved and suitable for both still and flowing water. A similar quill to the crow's is that of the goose. It is bulkier and heavier than the other floats

27

I have mentioned, and will usually be used for fishing flooded winter rivers, where a heavier float is an essential.

Then we have a quill not from a bird, but a porcupine. This quill will vary from about 2 in. to 10 in. long, and for anything but very light fishing is very good indeed – and quite durable if looked after. Many other floats are made from balsa wood, cane and cork, and they come in hundreds of different types and sizes. Those with long thin tops are called antenna floats and are very useful for fishing in windy conditions, while the ones with long, thin bottom sections and cork or balsa bodies are usually meant for trotting the stream. It is important to remember that you should always use the smallest float that conditions will allow. Don't fall into the trap of using floats as big as mooring buoys – you won't get any bites!

The last float I'll mention is the 'self-cocking' variety. This float does exactly what its name suggests – it will cock itself upright in the water without the addition of extra weight (shot) on the line. It is used mainly in still water, and makes an excellent rig for fishing slowly-sinking baits – which will be explained in greater detail later.

Floats are fixed to the line with float caps. These are small rings of rubber or plastic, tight enough to hold the float firmly in position, but free enough to allow the float to be slid up and down the line. I know it's only a very small item, but I advise you to get good quality float caps; having bought some good floats, you don't want to lose them at the first cast.

As already mentioned, most floats can be made to slide up and down the line by attaching the line through the metal ring at the bottom of the float. Using this method, deep water can be float-fished, the float being 'stopped' by the line at the right depth. Generally floats are fragile things and are best kept in a suitable container for protection during transit Tackle shops sell long float tubes and boxes for this purpose. Also, floats will always be the better for several coats of good waterproof varnish. This will prevent them from gradually absorbing water and sinking when they shouldn't.

Hooks: I have no hesitation in suggesting that the hook is the most important item of tackle in the angler's box. Unfortunately in many cases, the angler regards his hooks as the *least* important item. This is dangerous thinking, and you should remember that, no matter how perfect the rest of your tackle might be, a bad hook can spell disaster!

Hooks are available with three distinct types of line attachment: hooks to nylon, eyed hooks, and spade-end hooks, and whichever type you decide upon, get the very best that you can afford. Even highly-experienced anglers have some difficulty in recognising good hooks, and this is because the most crucial thing about a hook is its 'temper'. Tempering is the process which determines the hardness of the steel and, if the metal is too soft, the hook will pull out, or bend under strain. If it's too hard, it simply snaps, usually near the bend or the barb. So, without trying each individual hook, we must accept the maker's description. However, even good hooks are relatively cheap compared with some other items of the beginner's tackle, so I suggest that you pay more for good hooks – which will pay you in the long run.

The hook to nylon is probably the one the beginner will be attracted to first. This hook is tied to about 12 in. to 18 in. of nylon line, and comes packed in its own little packet. For some odd reason, the coil of line is usually most difficult to untangle and once this is achieved, the hook line is tied direct to your reel line by means of a loop provided. Actually, I have several basic criticisms of these hooks. They are expensive compared to loose hooks that you tie on yourself, and they tend to be tied to a somewhat heavier nylon than is really required for roach fishing. Also, on occasions, they are unreliably tied.

Summing up, hooks to nylon have some disadvantages, so I would suggest to you, as a beginner, that you consider the following two alternative types of hook. Firstly, the eyed hook – which is very easy to attach. As the name implies, it has an 'eye' or ring to allow the line to be tied directly to the hook. This eye can be a straight one, or bent away from the point of the hook (this is called an 'up-eyed') or bent towards the point, (when it is termed a 'down-eyed'). The same knot will successfully tie

29

all three types of eyed hook, and it is called the 'half blood' knot. The third main type of hook – and the one most used by the 'crack' angler – is the 'spade end' which, instead of an eye, has a flattened end. This hook is tied with a special knot, which together with the knot for eyed hooks, can be seen in the illustration on page 109. On the last hook, the 'spade' acts as a 'stop' to prevent the knot from slipping off the hook. When you first begin to try this knot, don't despair. Recently I taught six children, aged from six to eight, to tie good sound knots in only ten minutes!

When buying hooks, always look for a good sharp point and a small, neat barb that's not to big to prevent the hook from being struck home into the fish's mouth. Another thing to look for is a hook with a flattened bend, which strengthens the area receiving the most strain. The 'shank' or straight part of the hook can be long or short, but, as a beginner, choose the long shank; it is much easier to tie and easier to remove from the fish.

Hooks are available in a number of different thicknesses of wire and, for the roach angler, some fine wire hooks can be an advantage, for the thinner hooks are usually sharper and penetrate more easily. Their disadvantages are that they are slightly weaker, so choose your hooks with great care.

Hooks are also available in a wide variety of patterns: Crystal Bend, Round Bend, Limerick, Sproat, Inpoint, etc. They also come in several colours, like gold, silver, bronzed, blued, japanned, nickel, etc. To avoid bewilderment, let me recommend the following two types, to begin with:

1. A crystal hook, preferably with a dark colour finish, for use with maggots, hempseed, wheat, tares and breadcrust.
2. A round bend hook, again in a dark finish, for use with casters, worms, breadpaste and cheese.

You will note that, in general, if the hook has to be put into the bait, I recommend the round bend, but if the bait is to hang from the hook, I suggest the crystal. It's really a matter of bait presentation.

Hooks require special storage if the life, finish and sharpness is to be maintained; they must not be allowed to rattle around together, or get damp and rusty. A good tight-fitting tin lined with fine plastic foam is probably the best receptacle for loose hooks, while hooks to nylon can be stored in a plastic wallet made for the job. When you're fishing, always give your hooks constant checks, as the point can easily break off through contact with some hard object, like a stone, on the the bottom. *Small tackle:* this describes the multitude of small bits and pieces an angler needs to complete his tackle box. Firstly, the 'split-shot'. These are small lead weights used mostly by float fishermen to sink the bait and cock the float upright in the water, with just the right amount showing above the surface to register bites. They come in a range of sizes (largest first): Swanshot AAA, BB, 1,2,3,4,5,6,7,8. They are, in fact, shotgun shot sizes, stolen from the wildfowler, which is why the first one is called 'Swanshot'.

These little shots are split down the side to allow for attachment to the line, and they should always be soft enough for closing by finger-and-thumb pressure – and opened again with the fingernail. If split-shot is too hard, it's not only more difficult to attach, but can also damage the nylon line.

Shot comes in small packets or boxes, usually mixed sizes, but the most convenient pack is a 'dispenser' which is a plastic container, with several shot sizes in segmented compartments and a revolving punched top that dispenses one size without releasing the others. Leger leads are available in several different types and sizes, but to begin with I suggest you use only two, the 'drilled bullet' and the 'Arlesey Bomb'. Drilled bullets come in fractions of inches, e.g. $\frac{1}{8}$ in., $\frac{1}{4}$ in. and $\frac{1}{2}$ in. diameters. Arlesey Bombs have a metal swivel fixed into the top, and are bought by weight, i.e. $\frac{1}{8}$ oz., $\frac{1}{4}$ oz., $\frac{1}{2}$ oz. and $\frac{3}{4}$ oz. Unless you intend to fish very heavy water like a weirpool, avoid the temptation of using very heavy leads; the smallest leger lead that will allow easy casting and holding the current is the one to use. Remember that, with roach in particular, the explosion of a great lump of lead whistling into the water is enough to scare every fish in the river!

There are several devices for placing groundbait into the

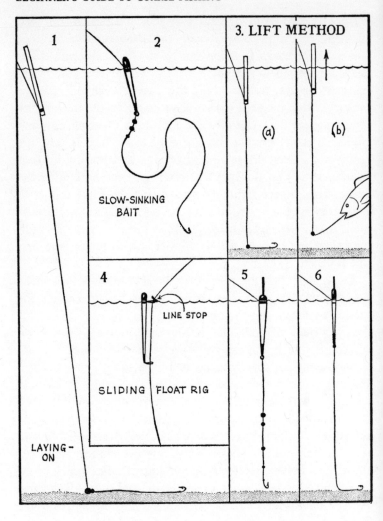

Shottings for various float tackles. (1) 'Laying-On' or float legering, with the weight (drilled bullet) heavier than the float. (2) Slowly-sinking bait method, with shot bunched close under the float (3) 'Lift' method, showing the float lifting when the fish takes the bait (4) Sliding float tackle, showing barrel knot 'stop' on line (5) Shotting for 'trotting the stream' in fast water (6) Self-cocking float rig, with coil of fine lead wire on the bottom of the float. (All hooks are shown unbaited, for clarity).

swim. For float fishing a 'dropper' is used, which is filled with bait, usually maggots or hemp, the lid closed and a trigger clipped shut. This is lowered to the riverbed, and when the trigger strikes the bottom it opens the lid and spills the bait into the swim. Once the swim has been baited, the dropper is removed from the line and a baited hook tackle cast out – over the groundbait. This is a very accurate method of groundbaiting.

Another good groundbaiter is the 'swimfeeder', which is a clear plastic tube, perforated and weighted, which can be filled with groundbait and used to help casting, particularly when legering at long distances. Once in the swim, the action of the water washes the groundbait out onto the riverbed, attracting fish to the baited tackle nearby. Closed-end swimfeeders are similar, but are normally used only for maggots; they have a cap fitted over each end to prevent the maggots escaping when casting.

There are at least six different types of bite indicator, but for reasons of clarity, I'll only recommend three of them to the beginner. Firstly, the 'swingtip', which is really a separately fitted extension to the rod, through which the reel line passes. It has a flexible coupling to the top rod-ring and, when in place, hangs down from the rod-top, bites being indicated by a fish tightening the line and lifting the swingtip. Another rod-extension indicator is the 'quivertip', which unlike the swingtip, is rigidly in line with the rod, when fitted. Bites are indicated by the quivertip's jerking or jumping action.

'Butt' indicators are fitted between the reel and the lowest, or butt rod-ring, and can consist of a slotted cork which clips over the line, or even a piece of stick, placed across the line and resting on the ground. As the bite has to register through all of the rod-rings before reaching the indicator, it is a considerably less sensitive method than either the swingtip or quivertip.

Rod-rests are an essential item for the roach angler, and they should be light, strong and practical. The best ones are made from strong aluminium alloy tube with tops of rubber-covered wire, which should always have a 'line drop' to allow the line to pass freely through the rod-rings when a fish takes. Telescopic or adjustable rod-rests are also available, but naturally they are more expensive.

The roach fisherman will need at least two types of net; a landing net and a keepnet. The most important of these is the landing net, which is used to land the fish, when it has been 'played' and is, preferably, lying on its side near the bank. Triangular folding-frame types are the best, with either a telescopic handle extending to about 7 ft, or with a simple one-piece handle roughly 5 ft long. When buying your landing net, get the best that you can afford, and look for a net-mesh made from non-rot nylon or terylene material, if possible.

Keepnets are used to retain fish after they've been caught – for 'weighing-in' at a contest, or, sometimes, to keep specimens for photographing or verifying by someone in authority. I have my own views on these nets and, in general, I do not recommend them, except for the express purposes mentioned above. Remember that even the largest keepnet can cause damage to a fish's fins and scales as he frantically fights for his freedom, and even if the fish are returned to the water later (which they should always be, unless dead), scale damage will almost surely result in disease and, finally, in the death of the fish. So, if you must have a keepnet, be sure to get one as large as possible, and always position it in a good depth of water, well out of hot sunshine.

Another useful item is a 'bank stick'. This is usually fitted with a standard thread, into which a keepnet or rod-rest can be screwed, and is very popular with match fishermen.

You will also need a 'disgorger', a device for removing the hook from a fish's mouth, particularly when that hook has been taken back into the mouth or 'tongue.' For the beginner, the most simple form is either a fork-end or tube-type disgorger, but other, more sophisticated types – like artery forceps – are used by many big-fish men.

Having equipped yourself with most of the basic items of tackle, including several rods, you will then need a good 'holdall', which is usually designed to carry rods, landing net handle and rod-rests. Your holdall should be made from a good waterproofed material and have a strong shoulder-strap, also a compartment for a fishing umbrella – which, for obvious reasons, is a very useful piece of equipment.

To accommodate all the small items, like bait boxes, reels, floats, your vacuum flask, etc., a good fishing bag or 'seat basket' should be considered, as many good fishing spots are a very long way from where the car or motorbike is parked. Whatever you buy for this purpose, be sure that this is light and comfortable to carry – and is protected against heavy showers.

Lastly, you will need a good fishing seat – if you haven't already purchased a seat-basket. Several types of light, folding, aluminium-framed seats are available, and whatever you choose, ensure that it has a strong, waterproof seat and is very light in weight. Remember that it has to be carried, like other tackle, sometimes over long distances. Try out your seat in the tackle shop, too – you're probably going to spend a considerable number of hours parked in it, so it might as well be as comfortable as possible.

FISHING METHODS

Now that you have a good idea about where roach are to be found, and the tackle and baits with which to catch them, let's get down to some serious fishing methods. Of these, float fishing is easily the most popular method and probably the most efficient one, but we should be familiar with the difference between float fishing on rivers and the same method in still waters.

River Fishing: fast- or even fairly slow-flowing waters require different fishing techniques to lakes and ponds. Firstly, you have to decide whether you're going to 'anchor' the bait on the bottom, or let the tackle swim down the stream, with the bait travelling anywhere between a few inches under the surface to actually just touching the riverbed. When float tackle is fished so that it travels with the current, it is called 'trotting the stream', so let's deal with this method first, as I believe more

35

water can be covered in this way and you can find out, easily and more quickly, where the roach are feeding.

Before starting to fish, always throw in a little groundbait. This helps to get the fish together, and they should then be all ready and waiting for you, when your baited tackle is presented. Let's imagine that you're going to use maggots for hookbait. Throw in a small handful of these, about the same distance out in the river as you intend to fish, but well upstream. The faster the current, the further upstream you will need to throw them, so that, when they reach near-bottom, they will be near to your fishing spot. Then put your tackle together. I usually stick my rod-rests in the bank first, then make up the rod, fix the reel on, feed the line through the rings, slide the float on (for medium to fast water I would use one with a cork body and a fair amount of buoyancy), and then tie a hook on the end of the line.

You must master this hook-tying art thoroughly before starting to fish seriously. You can use quite a fine nylon line for roach fishing – about 2 lb. breaking strain is right for most rivers – and you should always tie your hooks directly to the line, rather than use the hooks to nylon mentioned in the tackle section. Next, attach the split-shot to the line, under the float, and fix a plummet to the end of the tackle and cast out into the 'swim'. I must explain this term 'swim'. The area of water you've chosen to fish is always called a swim by anglers, so from now on, I'll simply say swim – without the quote marks.

While you're doing all this you'll find the rod-rest useful for parking the rod. Now, all ready? Put the landing net together, erect your seat, get the keepnet ready if you're using one, and put a second rod-rest in the bank, about 3 ft behind the first one. Gather your groundbait, nets, tackle box, vacuum flask, food, etc. around your chair. Put a couple of maggots on the hook (hook them lightly in the 'blunt' end) and cast. If you don't feel like casting from a sitting position, stand by all means, but sit down as soon as you've cast, for you're much less likely to scare the fish if your bulk is off the skyline.

A word about casting. For normal, fairly short-distance float fishing, my favourite – and an easy one for the beginner – is the simple 'underhand' cast. Here's how it's done, assuming that you're using a fixed spool reel. Holding the rod in one hand, grasp the baited tackle in the other hand, just above the hook, with just enough tension on the line to pull the rod-top over about three inches. Then open the bale-arm of the reel. with the same hand holding the line, keeping the tension at the same level, and swing the rod up with a steady underhand sweep, letting the baited line go at the right moment. When the tackle hits the water (with as little splash as possible), tighten up from the reel, which automatically closes the bale-arm.

Now toss a few maggots into the swim, by your float. For a start, fish your bait close to, or just tripping the bottom of the river – for that's where the best quality roach are usually to be found, and I'd like your very first fish to be a good one. You can try fishing the bait at different depths later, when you've got the hang of the preliminaries. Then, keeping the line as tight as possible, let the current carry the baited tackle downstream, following its progress with the tip of your rod. Never let the surface drift or current make large coils or bends in the line, and remember that, when you strike at a bite, you must pick up all the line quickly. So, the straighter the line between the rod and the float, the faster the strike will be.

When a bite does come, it will probably be the 'double knock' that is typical of a roach. The first 'knock' will just dip the float, very sharply, and, a second or two later, the second knock will arrive, which should be a firm plunging under of the float. Strike now – with a steady upward sweep of the rod. Don't swoosh it too hard or you'll have the tackle – and, maybe, a poor unsuspecting little fish – flying over your shoulder.

If you hook the fish on the strike, and it's a good one, let it run around for a bit, not towards dangerous snags though – and don't be in a hurry to get it on the bank. Get the 'feel' of a roach on the end of your line. When you feel that the fish is ready for landing, draw it gently upstream towards you, lower the landing net into the water and guide him over it, then net him with as little commotion as possible; you don't want to scare the whole shoal away.

37

Now, a word about unhooking fish. This will apply not only to roach but also to every species mentioned in this book. I've met many beginners who really love fishing but *hate* to unhook fish. I've watched them, sometimes, struggling to take a hook out of a fish, not wanting to hurt it, but nevertheless taking far too long over it, with the poor creature gasping its life away on the bank. You *must* be swift and firm. Get your disgorger or forceps to work, and take out the hook firmly and quickly – and don't be afraid to apply some deft pressure and leverage. Get used to doing this right away and you'll cause your fish much less pain. Remember, also, to wet your hands before handling any live fish; they're cold-blooded creatures, and hot, dry hands can cause them a lot of unnecessary discomfort.

Having unhooked the fish, be a sport and let him go! I really don't approve of keepnets myself, for they can do untold damage, particularly if the fish are all crammed in there together on a hot day, in very shallow water, where the oxygen content of the water is low. It's up to you. If you're fishing a 'match' or you've caught some big specimen roach worth recording, a keepnet is *just* permissible; otherwise forget it – just to please me!

Back to the fishing. Toss in a few more maggots, bait your hook, then cast out again. Swim down the stream, catch another roach, and so on. Now you're enjoying yourself and it isn't really so difficult is it? If the bites stop, or become very infrequent, try lowering the float down the line; the roach might have begun to feed higher in the water. Alternatively, change your bait. Perhaps a nice bit of new breadcrust will do the trick. You could, also, vary your casting distance, and try fishing further out into the river or closer to the bank. And you could even change your swim if things get very quiet. If you finally get tired of swimming the stream, or if the water is fast and coloured after some heavy rain, that is the time to try a spot of legering.

With this method, the float comes off the line and a heavier weight is attached, like a number of split-shot, a bored bullet or an Arlesey bomb. The amount of weight will be dictated by the speed and power of the current and, in very heavy water, a 'bomb' of up to one ounce could be necessary. Remember, however, that with this amount of weight you will need a stronger line than 2 lb. strength and, possibly, a heavier rod!

Normally, leger tackle can be cast further than float tackle, because of the increased weight. This means that the centre channels of the river may be explored – and, often, that is where the larger roach will be hiding. Using any of the baits previously described, cast your leger out, slightly downstream and, when the lead has settled on the bottom, tighten the line up to the rod-top and put the rod in the rests. The leger cast is somewhat different to the float fishing cast. Simply reel the baited tackle up to about 2 ft from the top of the rod, open the bale arm on the reel, keeping a finger on the spool to trap the line, then give a neat swing out, at about 45° angle, releasing your finger from the spool as the line leaves the reel. Do try to avoid the big, flashy overhead casts that some legermen use; they strain the tackle and causes a great splash when the lead hits the water.

There are several different ways of detecting bites on the leger. The simplest method – and one that I use myself quite a lot – is to stand the rod in a rod-rest at an angle of about 45°, then to settle in your seat and watch the rod-top like a hawk. Any roach bites will usually come as a 'knock-knock' on the tip of the rod, so strike at the second knock and ignore any small twitchings or tremblings – they'll probably be caused by bits of debris, weed or even fish, bumping against the line.

If you get fish right away, fine, otherwise I suggest that you search every part of the swim with your leger – downstream, upstream, out towards the opposite bank, or even close to your feet, particularly if the water is running fast and deep. For this type of legering, the 'quivertip' can be very effective, and, being a very flexible extension to the rod-top, it will pull round to an incredible extent, even if the bite is only from a very small fish. This method is beginning to gain great popularity among the 'match' or competition anglers, and it is very sensitive in still or very slow-running water; but, where the current is running at a fair speed, it cannot be used. The 'swingtip' is also good in slow

39

rivers, streams and canals. This rod extension indicator drops down on a tubular or solid plastic 'hinge' when the tackle is cast out, and bites are registered as the tip jumps up to become level with the rest of the rod. It can be used in fairly fast water, however, and by 'weighting' the end of the swingtip, it can be adjusted to all but very fast-flowing currents.

A general word of warning, however, when legering for roach. Don't be caught off your guard; big chub, barbel, bream, perch and other large fish can all fall to a legered roach bait – so watch out for fireworks on very light lines!

Stillwater Fishing: basically, all the tackle that you use for river fishing will do for still waters, but, because you have no strong current to contend with, everything can be 'scaled down' in weight. Finer lines, smaller hooks and lighter rods can be used, if necessary. And, although legering methods will be almost identical to those used in river fishing, for bite indication the more sensitive tip indicators should be used. Float fishing, however, takes on a different flavour, and I'll try to explain this in detail.

The biggest difference is that your float will not be moving, unless you're fishing off the bottom and there's an appreciable surface or wind drift on the water. The effects of wind and drift on still waters are usually counteracted by the use of special floats like the antenna types, which have their main 'bulk' under the surface, and display a long thin top above the waves.

In the main, the better-class stillwater roach are found on, or very close to, the bottom. So, even for the beginner, I'll recommend bottom fishing. In very hot, settled weather, the better roach could start feeding nearer the surface and, at these times, a slowly-sinking bait, descending finally to about mid-water, will take them. In bottom fishing, however, the main enemy to look for is weed. Some lakes and ponds are covered with the stuff, from light, feathery surface weed to the thick, cabbagy growths that can spell disaster to fine tackle.

Fish *are* taken right down into the bottom weed, but your chances of locating them are slim – unless the water is so crammed with fish that you drop your bait on their noses at every cast! Generally, you should aim to settle your bait gently on top of the weed and, when 'shotting' your tackle, you should make sure that the shots are attached well *up* the line, near the float, leaving a good, weightless 'trail' of line with the baited hook at the end. The shotting diagrams on page 32 will help to make this clear.

Remember the weed when you are fishing heavier baits like breadpaste. Very few lakes are completely covered with it, so that it will pay you to seek out a fishing spot which has, at least, a weed-free area or two. In lake fishing, the plummet is an essential item of tackle. This cone-shaped weight should be attached to the hook by passing the line through its eye, and then bringing the hook under the plummet into the small cork wedge underneath. Set the float to the estimated depth with the plummet attached, cast out, and let the tackle settle. If the float is too high on the line, it will lay flat on the surface of the water, so drop it down the line and cast again, until it is just 'cocked' in the water at the right height, with enough tip showing to register a bite. Once the correct depth has been found, take the plummet off and bait the hook, ready for fishing. If you have carried out this operation accurately, your baited hook should be just touching the bottom. Then attach your weight or shots, which will take the place of the plummet in cocking the float at the right depth.

At this point, we come to the explanation of two different float-fishing methods for bottom fishing. The first method is called 'laying-on'. It depends on the amount of weight that will actually sink the float when the hook is off the bottom of the lake. The best weight for laying-on is a small bored bullet, stopped on the line by a single small split shot. The length of 'trail' between the weight and hook can vary, but for general conditions it will be about 6 in. to 12 in. With this method, you can easily adjust the correct fishing depth without a plummet; you simply make up the tackle, with float, bullet, split-shot and hook, and estimate the depth and cast out, just as you did with the plummet. You should adjust the weight until the float is cocked in the water at about 45°, then reel in, pull the float *up* the line about 3 in. or so, bait the hook and cast. When the rod is settled in the rest, you'll find that the float is lying flat on the surface (because you took it up the line a little), so reel in gently until the float is nicely cocked. This should give you a good, almost straight line between rod-top and bait, ready for a quick strike when a bite arrives. This 'laying-on' rig will not work in very fast water, but according to the amount of weight used, will still hold nicely in medium to slow streams.

The second method is known as the 'lift' method and is probably one of the most popular and efficient ways of float-fishing in still waters, as apart from roach, it works just as well for other species like tench, bream and crucian carp. Almost any lightweight float will do, but in my view the peacock quill is unrivalled for this method, and preferably a piece about 5 in. long, although much shorter lengths are used by many experienced roach anglers. Having slid a float on the line and attached a hook, roughly estimate the amount of shot required to cock the float upright in the water, with about $\frac{3}{4}$ in. of tip showing above the surface, or more in windy conditions. At first, use too little shot, adding more until the float cocks as described. To adjust it to very fine limits (as it should be) you will be wise to attach the shot 'loosely' at first, that is, pinched on the line just tight enough to hold. Two or three practice casts later, you might find that the float is still showing too much tip above water, so simply slide the shot *up* the line, very carefully, until the correct amount of tip is visible. Ideally, the shot (and I rarely use more than two), should be bunched together, so that they are resting on the bottom, with a trail of line, from shot to hook, no more than 2 in. long.

This makes an extremely sensitive rig, and when a fish takes the bait, the shot is lifted off the bottom – causing the float to 'lift' in the water, visibly. That's how the methods gets its name. With fairly shy-biting fish like big roach, the bite should be struck on the slightest 'lift' of the float, but where bites are more pronounced, the 'lift' will usually develop into the float actually rising out of the water and finally laying flat for about two seconds, when it slides under and away.

Groundbaiting in still waters is a slightly different proposition to that in rivers and streams. Unless the lake you're fishing is particularly windy, your groundbait will stay where you throw it, so it can, therefore, be of a much lighter consistency – and less of it – than river groundbait. In some good roach lakes, a nice 'cloud' groundbait, as mentioned in the section on roach baits, brings the fish to feed very well.

Hempseed fishing requires a somewhat different technique to normal float fishing on both still and fast-flowing waters. Generally, the tackle should be as light as possible, with a hook no larger than no. 14, and a small crow quill float. The tackle should be weighted with a small coil of soft lead wire, just under the bottom ring of the float, as ordinary split-shot looks too much like actual hempseed grains (it's about the same size and colour). With this method, most of the bites will come as soon as the bait hits the water, so be prepared – bites on hemp will be sharp and very fast, so your striking reflexes must match, but be careful, some very big roach come to this bait and although the strike should be quick, it must be tempered with a certain amount of care, particularly as lines for hemping are usually no stronger than 2 lb.

One of the small 'self-cocking' floats can be used for hemp fishing; one which has the weight built into the bottom, but my experiences with these floats have proved that every little up, down, sideways or across movement should be struck.

Groundbaiting with hempseed should be on the principle of 'little and often' and I usually throw out about a dozen grains for every two or three casts. One last thing; before you fish with hemp, make sure that it's allowed on that particular water, as some clubs have banned it.

CHAPTER 2

Rudd

This pretty red-finned fish is not as widely distributed through-out the country as the roach. It is more a creature of lake, pond and canal than the fast-flowing river, and is not often found north of the border. It also prefers weedy waters, and some good catches have been made from Slapton Ley in Devon, the Norfolk Broads system, the Cheshire meres and many lakes and rivers in Southern Ireland.

A rudd of $1\frac{1}{2}$ lb. is a specimen – a feather in the cap for the lucky angler, but in some southern counties they're often taken up to about $2\frac{3}{4}$ lb. But you, my friend, just starting at the game, should regard a one-pound rudd as a very good fish indeed.

Many specialists will tell you that big rudd are nearly always caught on or close to the bottom; well, I'm not a rudd *expert*, but I've had several up to $2\frac{1}{2}$ lb. and some of the larger ones were caught very close to the surface, using tactics which I'll describe later. So, in general, look upon your rudd as a surface, or near surface, feeder. Maybe there's a farm pond near you that's teeming with rudd. Well, get down there one sunny morning in summer and you'll see what I mean, hundreds of them will be 'sporting around' on the surface, taking flies and other insects – you can't fail to spot them.

Rudd are happy, busy little fish, and when conditions suit them, they're so efficient at increasing their numbers, they will literally 'take over' a water and while they won't always be big ones, you'll be able to catch them 'till the cows come home'.

Also, they mix happily with other fish like roach and tench, and where rudd and pike exist in the same water, both species will often run large; the pike growing big and fat on the rudd, and the rudd – with less competition for food – will also make a good average size.

Rudd and roach will sometimes produce a hybrid or 'cross-breed' and on the odd occasion I've seen this, they've proved to be handsome, hard fighting fish and well worth going after. Sometimes, you'll even find the rudd used as an ornamental fish for garden or park ponds, where their bright colouring and perky behaviour delights the spectators.

Baits: most of the roach baits will do for rudd, particularly bread and maggots, and remembering what I was just saying about surface feeding, always fish your bait closer to the surface than you would for roach – and don't be afraid to try natural baits, like a good buzzy bluebottle (easily obtained by letting maggots hatch out in a tin) which has accounted for some good sized fish.

Fishing a floating natural or artificial fly on the surface can also take rudd, and I'll be discussing this method later, very briefly, I'm afraid, as fly-fishing requires an instruction book all it's own. I'll also be showing you how to take rudd on floating breadcrust.

Where rudd grow to a good size in rivers, or when the weather gets colder on lakes and ponds, then you should fish for them on or nearer to the bottom. And here's a good tip. Try the bottom half of a lively lobworm, or a couple of marsh worms – you could get top-class rudd that way, but watch out for perch, bream, barbel or anything else that's in the same water; in other words, use slightly heavier tackle than you would for surface fishing.

Groundbaits for surface-feeding rudd should be lightly mashed bread, breadcrumb 'cloud', loose maggots (if you're using them on the hook) or anchored breadcrust, a method that will be fully explained later.

Tackle: your roach tackle will do very nicely for rudd, but you should invest in a 'bubble' float – a small plastic sphere which can be filled with water. This acts as a floating weight on the line (for casting purposes) and looks just like a little natural bubble when it's on the surface. The amount of water you put in the bubble determines its depth in the water, and if filled entirely, with one split-shot added, it makes an ideal method for legering on top of fine weed in lakes and rivers.

Methods: rudd fishing can be roughly divided into two sections; surface and near-surface fishing, and bottom fishing. In general, the first method applies mainly to lakes and ponds, and the second to medium and fast-flowing waters. Methods for bottom fishing, that is with float tackle and a bait lying on the bottom, or legering, swingtipping, quiver-tipping, or using one of the other bite indicators, will be virtually the same as for roaching.

The bubble float, as described in the tackle section, will be fished on ordinary roach tackle, and is deadly when fished near areas of thick water-lilies. The best bait for this method, in my own experience, is breadcrust – about the size of a half new penny. Before fishing the bubble, scatter a few small pieces of bread on the surface, near to where you're going to fish, to attract the rudd to your bait. Be careful if big carp inhabit the same water though, you might find a furious fight on your hands – and possibly some broken tackle!

A small artificial fly can also be fished on bubble tackle, but my preference is for a live fly like a bluebottle or even a lively house fly. With this method, the rod should be held all the time, and some movement imparted to the fly, from time to time, by reeling in a foot of line, or 'trembling' the rod-top. On the Norfolk Broads, big bags of rudd can be made by anchoring a boat against the reeds and fishing the bubble, baited with bread, right up against the reed-bed about ten to twenty yards away.

CHAPTER 3

Perch

Like the roach, the spritely, striped, red-finned perch is found in most parts of the British Isles in almost any type of water you can imagine, from reservoirs, lakes, ponds, canals, pits, streams, rivers – even tiny farm ponds.

He's a greedy biter and a fast, efficient breeder and, where he exists in large numbers, he will take an angler's bait right through the fishing season. Time seems not to matter to the perch; hot sultry afternoons, crisp, smoky autumn mornings – even hard winter days when the water's fringed with ice – it's all the same to him.

The very first fish the new angler catches is quite likely to be a perch, for what an obliging character he is! He'll take a wide variety of baits, at almost any depth and the bite, when it's on float tackle, will be unmistakable. Your float will be dancing down the swim with a juicy worm or large bunch of maggots on the hook, when it will suddenly jiggle, bob under, run along the surface then dive under; no mistaking it – bang! Strike! – he's on!

Once you find your perch, there's sure to be more, maybe even one after the other, almost 'queuing up' to get caught. Mind you, it isn't quite like that with the larger ones over $1\frac{1}{2}$ lb. or so. No, you'll have ro really *fish* for those and they won't come in large numbers, but don't worry, if you fancy getting to grips with some big 'uns, I'll be dealing with them later on.

Most of your perch are going to be between about 2 oz. and

8 oz., and if you should land one of $1\frac{1}{2}$ lb., you have yourself a specimen. Push the weight up to $2\frac{1}{2}$ lb. to 3 lb. and you're in the big time. Anything over 4 lb. could get your picture in the paper!

But in the beginning, I suggest you find yourself a water full of small to medium sized perch and 'wean' yourself on those. Later, if there's any adventure in your soul, you'll seek out a big gravel pit or river where perch run large, and then go after some real rod-benders. There's no mistaking the presence of perch, particularly big ones. They usually chase shoals of small roach, dace, minnows, sticklebacks, etc., and when feeding, can be seen scattering the small fry all over the surface. Small to medium perch will hunt in packs, but the larger ones (over about 2 lb.) prefer deeper, more sheltered water, where they lurk, waiting to pounce on a good-sized fish meal. They are usually 'lone wolves', prefering to hunt alone and, because of this, are much more difficult to locate.

A few of the more obvious perch waters spring to mind; Oulton Broad in Suffolk (not as good as it used to be), Arlesey Lake in Bedfordshire, the middle reaches of the Hampshire Avon, and a select few stretches of the Suffolk Stour. Some huge perch lurk in a few city reservoirs, but they are difficult to catch owing to the vast expanses of water to search. The best conditioned perch will generally be found in clean, unpolluted water as they are, in fact, prone to an infection which, on occasions, has wiped out entire perch populations in various lakes, ponds and rivers.

Baits: any hook bait that moves, wriggles, flashes or swims will take perch, but generally, of you're fishing for the average-sized ones, a worm takes some beating as an all round bait. In my own experience, the bigger the bait, the bigger the perch has not been a bad principle, with a few notable exceptions – when a tiny perch gobbled up a huge lobworm, for example.

So try lobworms, brandling worms, marsh worms or maggots for a start, just to get some experience. Then, when you feel more confident, start using live or dead fish baits to tempt the heavier specimens. Minnows, gudgeon, bleak or tiny roach, dace or rudd will all attract perch, particularly if fished at mid-water on moving float tackle. Fish baits can also be fished on the bottom, and where really big perch exist, you can even use small sprats or coarse fish up to about six inches long. My own best perch was 4 lb. 2 oz. from Oulton Broad – and it took a live-baited roach 7½ in. long!

Another bait worth considering is a small frog, fished and worked fairly close to the surface, but whatever you do, don't use the poor little thing live, with hooks stuck all over him; he should be quickly killed first, then mounted on the tackle. I've also caught perch with breadpaste and other baits, even cheese, but this has been when fishing for other species. It really all adds up to the fact that our friend the perch will take almost anything!

The only 'groundbaiting' required when perch fishing will be a small amount of bread 'cloud', thrown into the water every few minutes. This isn't meant for the perch, but for the hoards of small silvery fry that, in turn, will entice the perch into your swim.

Tackle: again, your roach tackle will fill most of the requirement for perch fishing; and the hollow fibreglass rod, fixed spool reel and general float gear will be more than adequate. You'll need to step up your line strength however, as perch are less 'delicate' with a bait than roach, and are equipped with strong teeth. For legering, use a line of about 6 lb., as long-distance casting and striking places quite a strain on any tackle.

For float-fishing, use a larger float than you would for roach, preferably something with a cork body that will take two or three BB shot to cock it in the water. Hook size too should be larger, say a size 10 for bunches of maggots and small worms, and a size 6 to 8 for larger worms and single lip-hooked small livebaits, like minnows. When float fishing for perch, it will pay to keep the bait moving, continually, and if bites are not forthcoming, search the swim thoroughly, trying the bait at different depths until you find where they are.

For legering, using worms or small live or dead fish, a bored bullet or small 'bomb' will be needed, according to the casting

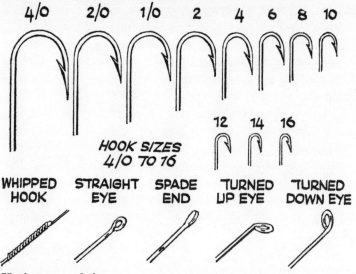

Hook types and sizes.

distance required, or the strength of the current. The ideal bite indicator for this type of legering is the 'butt' type, and always remember to give the perch plenty of time before striking; once they have taken a bait, they seldom reject it. A word of warning. Many perch waters contain pike, and if this is the case, I suggest you use a wire trace to the hook, say a length of about 6 in. to 9 in. Anything but very large pike should, with reasonable skill, be landed on this tackle.

A very useful item of gear for the perch angler is a minnow trap, which is baited with fine breadcrumbs and placed in the water near where small fry abound. This trap can catch minnows, sticklebacks, loaches and very small coarse fish of various species. These baits are fished on 'drop minnow' tackle, and the little dead fish is mounted on a leaded treble hook with its head pointing downwards. It can be fished on ordinary roach tackle, but without a float. Here's how it's done: cast out the bait, preferably after using a little 'cloud' groundbait to attract lots of small fry into the swim; let the bait settle just on the bottom, then retrieve in short jerks, to imitate the action of a dying fish. No bites? Never mind, cast and retrieve again, in a different place this time, until the swim has been well covered. This method is known as 'sink and draw', and can be deadly for taking perch; it also takes pike, so be careful.

On a crisp autumn day, when perch really start to move around, you could try a spot of spinning. Using your leger rod and fixed spool reel, attach a spinner to the end of the line. This can be any one of the smaller types available in the tackle shop, but preferably a 'reflex' spinner – one in which the 'blade' revolves around the bar of the hook. Spinning is inclined to put kinks into nylon line, which can be an awful nuisance, so I advise the use of a 'swivel' and an 'anti-kink' device.

Swivels allow the lure (spinner) to revolve without imparting a spinning movement to the line itself, and for perch fishing, using small spinners, the swivel should be correspondingly small. They come with useful 'clip' attachments on one end, and this should be fixed to the 'eye' of the spinner. Your line is tied to the other end of the swivel. Even with this device, some 'spin' can still get through the line, so you should then fit your anti-kink vane. This vane, which is often made from celluloid or some other transparent material, counteracts the spin by 'reversing' the direction of the line twist, and is well worth using for all types of spinning.

Very small plugs are worth trying too, and all these lures, with their appropriate methods of attachment, are shown in the various diagrams and photographs.

Methods: although I didn't mean to, I seem to have described dead-baiting and spinning for perch in some detail, in the last section, so I'll now talk about live-baiting, and legering.

Just to finalise on spinning however, a word about casting. The light spinning cast, when made from a typical leger or spinning rod and a fixed spool reel, should be a sharp 'up-and-over' movement, starting with the lure, or spinner, dangling from the rod-top about six inches. Detailed casting instruction is, unfortunately, beyond the scope of a beginner's book like this one, so please, get plenty of practice at casting – try it out on the lawn at home, or in a park when nobody is around, and *without* a hook on the line.

You can, of course, use ordinary roach float tackle for perching, and if you do, remember what has been said previously about keeping the bait on the move. The best baits for this are worms or even bunches of maggots. Small live fish can also be used on suitable float tackle, but this comes into the category of 'live-baiting', which I'll now explain.

When fishing a small live fish, and for perch, I would recommend a minnow or a very tiny roach or dace. The hook size should be at least a no. 6, and a float of the cork-bodied type fixed to the line. Always fish it high in the water, and move the bait around continually, searching all the likely places where perch lurk – like under bridge arches, on the edges of weedbeds or around poles and other water obstructions. If your livebait dies on you, or gets very limp, put a fresh one on – It's movement that counts when perching. For keeping your baits fresh, use a keepnet with a very fine mesh, or a plastic bucket filled with water and kept well out of the sun.

When legering for perch you can use a good lively lobworm, a small bunch of brandling or marsh worms, or perhaps a small dead fish. If there is some deep water around, try those places first, particularly in cold weather, and even with worms, try to keep the bait 'moving', if only very slowly, to attract the perch.

CHAPTER 4

Bream

There are two types of freshwater bream, the bronze or common bream and the silver bream. At the baby stage it will be difficult to spot the difference, but as they grow (and they're often found together) the bronze becomes darker in colour, while the silver – yes, you've guessed it – becomes silvery, shading to a light greenish brown on the back and shoulders.

Sometimes, you'll find bream in Scotland and the border counties but in the main, most of them reside south of the border. Like perch and roach, they're happy in most still and running waters, but if anything, prefer deepish waters with not too strong a flow. Typical 'breameries' are the rivers and broads of Norfolk and the Fens; the rivers Trent, Ouse and Medway, the Cheshire Meres and many other rivers, lakes, pits, ponds, canals and reservoirs throughout England and Ireland. In particular, some Essex and Kent waters hold very good bream, while in Ireland, the Shannon system of loughs and rivers probably provides the best all-round breaming in Europe.

A silver bream of 1 lb. is a big fish by most standards, and a two-pounder exceptional. If you take one over $4\frac{1}{2}$ lb., you'll be famous. Most of the time you'll get them in the 2 oz. to 8 oz. class, when they're called 'skimmers' in certain parts of the country. These are often fished for specially by competition anglers who catch lots of them to make up their match weights. Bronze bream reach a much larger size and 12 lb. to 13 lb. is now being realised on some waters, although these weights are exceptional. I've heard several stories in recent years about big bream seen that could run up 20 lb. or more, and one such place is Abberton Reservoir in Essex, a vast water where huge shoals of them are in residence.

In days past, some very large bream were taken from the Tring reservoirs in Hertfordshire, and although these seem to have lain 'dormant' for many years, they're now beginning to show up again, although the average size is not as large as it was.

In such waters, and in the larger rivers, bream are essentially shoal fish and will move around all day – and often all night – gobbling up the natural feed as they go, continually eating and moving on. That's why they're often difficult to locate, particularly on larger expanses of water.

If you're fishing a water like that, it will pay you to forget the tackle for a while and give the lake or river a thorough 'reccy' first. When you find a feeding shoal, you'll see them right enough, rolling or 'priming' on the surface, while others below them churn the water into a muddy cloud. Early morning at first light is an ideal time for this type of activity and when you locate them, get as much groundbait in as you can, to hold them in that spot as long as possible.

Baits: most roach baits will catch bream, they're not at all fussy once they're on the feed and bread baits, maggots or worms are probably the most popular baits. But here's a very good tip and one that has earned me many good bags of bream when ordinary baits have failed. It's quite simple really and I call it a bread and worm 'cocktail'. Simply put a nice piece of new white bread-crust on the hook, leaving the point of the hook well exposed, then hook a lively brandling or marsh worm on and presto! the famous cocktail. You *must* try that one, preferably fished on 'slow sinking' tackle.

Groundbaiting for bream is important, but be careful on this point as it's not permitted on some waters, mainly public reservoirs. Otherwise, of all the coarse fish, the bream is the one most likely to be taken in numbers with the help of generous groundbaiting, unless the water is a very, very small one. Bread, bran, middlings, meals, etc. all make a good mix, and you'll probably need to include some soft, cloudy stuff that will linger at midwater, plus some heavier 'gunge' that will hold bottom long enough to keep a big crowd of bream interested.

In fast rivers you can leave out the very soft stuff, it will only be carried away by the current anyway. In these conditions, it will pay to cup the groundbait around a couple of small stones to help it down to the bottom. Another thing, don't forget to put a good sprinkling of the hook bait into the groundbait – maggots, breadcrust, worms – whatever you decide to use.

Tackle: again, your roach rod and reel will fit the bill for bream, unless you're specifically going after fish over 7 lb., when a carp rod will be required. Hook sizes will be larger than for roach, say sizes from 12 to 6, and a little stronger line should be fitted, 4 lb. to 6 lb. is about right. Most of your larger roach floats will do for breaming, but if you're serious, invest in an antenna float and a sliding float for fishing rough and deeper water. These two methods will be described in detail later.

Landing nets and keepnets for bream should always be large, and as a lot of groundbait will usually be required, you'll need a couple of canvas or plastic buckets to carry it in. Only mix up enough groundbait for immediate requirements though, keep the bulk of it 'dry' for use throughout the day. You'll see the sense in this if you try humping 14 lbs. or more of wet groundbait around the bank – or over stiles. Bream leger tackle will be as for roach, but again, make the 'terminal' tackle (line, weight and hook) a little more substantial.

Methods: somehow, I always see the ideal bream water as a large lake with beds of dense reed or bullrush at the edges, with a few fishing spots cut into the bankside. My pals in the Fenland and Broadland river areas will probably quarrel with me on this point, as they will see their bream as typical slow moving river-dwellers, but never mind, we're both right.

When we get down to actual fishing methods however, we must draw the same distinction between river and stillwater fishing as we did for roach, and all the roach methods already described will apply equally well, with a few small exceptions, to both bronze and silver bream, the latter in particular.

Bronze bream can run quite heavy as I've already said, so if you're using your roach rod and reel, step up the hook size to anything from 12 to 6 and use a line of at least 4 lb. I must make it clear that this applies to 'pleasure' fishing of course, not competition angling where tiny hooks and gossamer lines are the order of the day.

Bream love deep 'holes' in lakes and rivers, and since many very deep flooded gravel pits have been stocked with bream over a period of years, you could find yourself fishing in twenty feet of water, or more. This is where the sliding float (as mentioned in the tackle section) really comes into its own. This float, which usually has a cork body, is fitted with an eyed ring to the centre or shoulder of the body, plus the usual bottom ring, and is allowed to slide freely up and down the line. Once the depth of water has been determined (by using a plummet), a line 'stop' is made by attaching a separate small length of heavier nylon monofilament, or a slip of rubber, on the line at the correct depth. This acts as a stop when the float travels up the line, after casting and settling, and the line should then be tightened from the reel, until the floats 'cocks' on the water at the right angle. When casting this rig, the float will naturally drop down to rest against the first shot on the line, and a smooth 'up-over-and-across' cast, similar to that used for legering, should be made.

Bream baits should be larger than those used for roach, and the previous notes about larger keepnets and landing nets must be remembered. In terms of popularity, legering and float-fishing methods seem to enjoy almost equal status in most parts of the country, but my own experience tells me that, with a few exceptions, the larger bream are taken on the leger.

When you've located a good shoal of bream, get plenty of groundbait in right away, if it's allowed. Use the heavier stuff for fast water and a much lighter mix for lakes, ponds, pits and canals. All the previously mentioned baits and groundbaits can be used, but my own preference is for new breadcrust on the hook, or a bunch of from four to six maggots. With all coarse fish, the recommendation of particular baits can be a very uncertain business, and I hesitate to do it; fish become used to different baits on different waters, and some bream go for worms, others prefer maggots, while some bream fisheries are exclusively bread waters.

In both lakes and still waters, bream will often feed at different levels in the water, with quite large fish moving around midwater – even close to the surface. On numerous occasions I've seen huge packs of them, notably on the Suffolk Waveney and one particular immense lough in County Clare, rolling or 'porpoising' with dorsal fins actually breaking the surface.

In situations like these, a slowly sinking bait could prove to be a real killer, and this method is quite a simple one. You could use a 'self-cocking' float, one with the weight at the bottom or *in* the bottom, or, as an alternative, move your split-shot right up to or just under the bottom ring on the float. If you have maggot, breadpaste or worm on the hook, these baits usually provide enough weight to allow a nice, naturally slow descent into the water, but breadcrust, because of its buoyancy, will need the addition of a small 'dust' shot on the line, not less than 3 in. from the hook.

Very often, bream are 'finnicky' biters anyway, so with the slow-sinking bait method, you need to watch the tackle like a hawk. Look for any sideways movement of the float that could signal a bite, or in flowing water, strike if the float *stops* or travels an inch or two upstream or across the stream.

For legering, the swingtip and quivertip are widely used, but for really heavy flowing water it will be pay to use a butt indicator, as already described. Another good method is to put the rod in one rod-rest, at an angle of 45°, and watch for 'thumps' on the tip of the rod. Three years ago last June, I reached the river Shannon near Athlone for a fishing holiday, only to find that majestic river in full flood. However, using a big lobworm on a no. 6 hook, with a one-ounce Arlesey bomb for weight, I caught 22 bronze bream over $2\frac{1}{2}$ lb. each, legering downstream almost into the bank, and watching the rod-top for bites.

Having got used to the sharp 'knock-knock' bites of roach, and the steady takes of perch and chub, you might find the average bream bite, on float tackle, a little disconcerting at first. These fish will often 'play around' with the bait, taking it delicately into the lips and blowing it out again, and on occasions, even swimming or backing away a few inches before rejecting it. This causes some very odd movements to the float, like little dips and tiny runs, so if you experience bites like those, keep your head and wait for a good take or run. Experience will tell you all.

In windy weather, the antenna float should be used, preferably one with an adjustable body that allows the amount of tip above water to be altered at will. This is a very sensitive rig and when the water gets really rough, as it will on big open lakes and Fenland rivers, the body should be slid right down to the bottom float ring. With the centre of gravity as low as possible, this float will 'ride' the waves nicely, and provide a sensitive indicator at the same time.

The match fishing fraternity have a jargon all their own when it comes to floats, and around the competitions you'll hear names like 'zoomers', 'darts', 'onions', 'missiles' and 'sticks' mentioned. Most of these floats have some merit in the particular conditions for which they're used, and although I'm not too keen on match fishing, I'll own that a lot can be learned from these crack competition anglers – knowledge that could be successfully applied to general coarse fishing.

Bream can be caught in summer and winter on most waters, but in summer, a dawn start will usually prove worthwhile. A 'dreamy, breamy day', commencing at first light and ending with a big netful of fish, will be an experience to remember, and you'll probably become addicted to bream, as I have.

CHAPTER 5

Carp

With the exception of pike and salmon, carp grow to the largest size of any freshwater fish in Britain. For this reason, they are surrounded by legend and mystery.

You've probably already heard some 'carp that got away' stories and might even have seen a few impressive press pictures of smug anglers in 'jungle' hats, cradling immense carp by the side of some well-stocked private lake. Well, without trying to dampen your enthusiasm, I must tell you that ordinary, every-day carp fishing isn't quite like that. While it's true that some very large carp are caught every season, it's also natural that they should hit the headlines, but take it from me, headlines apart, it often takes hours of concentrated preparation and fishing to produce one big carp. I even know of highly ex-perienced carp men who have fished for a *whole week* on a water known to hold very big carp, without even getting one bite for their trouble!

But don't be discouraged if the 'big stuff' is beyond your reach. You're new to fishing and you'd be well advised to tackle something a little smaller – and easier to catch.

Basically, there are only three types of British carp, none of them actually 'natives' of this country, but all imported from abroad at one time or another. The facts and figures on precisely when they were introduced are a little uncertain, but we do know that many years ago, the monks stocked their lakes and 'stew ponds' with carp from the European mainland. In this way, they fulfilled their religious requirement of eating fish on certain days, and provided themselves with some good sport as a bonus.

It would appear that, generally, these early arrivals were what are known today as 'wild' carp: slim, chub-shaped fish with full scaling and seldom reaching more than 10 lb. Even now, a 6 lb. 'wildie' would be something to shout about. This wild fish, which still inhabits a few English waters, is a really game fighter at the end of a line, and for sheer thrills and satisfaction, I can't recommend it too highly to the beginner.

But back to the history of the carp. After a while, the monks sought a larger, fast-growing variety of carp to provide even bigger meals and better sport, and so the 'King' carp was imported, again from Europe. This carp was a much heavier and more bulky specimen altogether, and quickly grew to a large average size, finding the muddy, weedy moats and ponds of England very much to their liking. When hooked, they showed great stamina and sporting ability, and about that time, eminent statesmen, even royalty, fished for them.

Although these king carp were a single species, they developed in different conditions and over a number of years, a variety of odd scale patterns which eventually became known to the modern angler as three separate fish; the mirror carp, leather carp and fully-scalled common carp. To complicate matters even further, cross-breeding occurred between the scale-types and it even became possible for the king carp to 'breed back' into wild carp after two or three generations.

Besides the King, another attractive little carp, the crucian, was introduced, which happily shared waters with its larger brothers and is still with us today, mainly in the Midlands and Southern England. This handsome and sporting little fish will reach a weight of 4 lb. in some waters, but this is exceptional, and a good average on most crucian waters is about $\frac{1}{2}$ lb. On suitably light tackle, he's a plucky little fighter and we'll be saying more about him later. The larger common and mirror carp will attain weights of from 20 lb. to 30 lb. in the right environment, and the record stands at 44 lb.

Various other strains of carp found their way into our waters over the years. These are the ornamental varieties like higoi, golden orfe and different types of goldfish, some of which, in the wild state, grow quite large and provide the angler with very good sport. If you should ever be lucky enough to have permission to fish a strictly private water holding these beautiful ornamental fish, it will always be good policy to return any you might catch, as quickly and carefully as possible; I'm sure the owners will thank you for it.

Well, that's how it all seems to have happened, but much later, during the savage winter of 1963 in fact, many of our 'native' carp perished beneath the unusually thick ice. As a result, we had to look to Europe again to replenish the stocks, and more carp were imported from various parts of the world. These were mostly 'basic' strains as we know them, but in some cases they were specialised – carefully cross-bred types from sophisticated fish-farms, bred especially for their fast rate of growth and improved resistance to extreme conditions of climate.

With few exceptions, these fish have adapted well to our British waters, providing a good head of carp in many waters which had not previously held them. So what was, in 1963, a deep tragedy for British angling, proved in the long term to be of great benefit, for today, thanks to proper breeding and re-stocking policies by clubs and individuals, there are more carp than ever before – and all this in spite of ever-encroaching industrial pollution.

Most of the carp described here will be found in lakes, ponds, gravel or sand pits and a few reservoirs throughout England and Wales. Ireland also have a few carp waters and no doubt they will find their way into more Scottish waters, when a strain is found that will withstand the extremely low winter temperatures north of the border. Generally then, look for them in still waters, particularly where there's a reasonably rich growth of aquatic plants and a muddy bottom. But don't ignore slow-moving rivers and canals; some rivers like the lower Thames, the Nene at Peterborough and the Somerset Brue have held big carp for some years, and more and more angling clubs are experimenting with the introduction of carp to fairly fast-flowing waters.

Baits: until fairly recently, baits for carp were almost confined to bread and worms, and while I personally believe, through my own experiences, that bread, particularly in crust form, is the best all-round bait, some more experimental baits like swan mussel, small whole potatoes and even meat baits such as tinned catfood, sausage meat and luncheon meat have already taken full honours on many established carp fisheries.

While this is all very interesting, I must confess that I find the question of many coarse fishing baits can easily become something of a 'cult', especially with the highly experienced specimen-hunters, so if I were you, I'd restrict myself to breadpaste, breadcrust and small potatoes, just for a start. The only exception would be when you're fishing a carp water that's hardly ever fished and never has bread thrown to the ducks. This is an unlikely possibility today, but if you do find such a place, then use big lobworms or bunches of smaller worms on your hook, according to the size of carp you're after. But once again, watch out! Lakes like that often contain big eels – which are very partial to a juicy worm legered on the bottom.

In waters where the carp continually patrol the surface, the best all-round bait is undoubtedly floating breadcrust, but make sure it's fresh, but not too new; about three days old is the ideal as it should then have the right buoyancy in the water. Carp have a very keen sense of smell, so your bait should always be completely free from odours like tobacco and petrol, etc.

For groundbait, several small pieces from the same loaf should be cast into the water where you're going to fish, but do this very carefully and gently, for carp are shy, wily creatures! If you take your crust from the outside of the loaf, make sure the white side is floating downwards in the water. Remember, it's this part the carp will see, and be attracted to, first.

Bread pastes for bottom fishing can be made in the usual way, with clean, white stale bread, and if you feel like experimenting, try adding your own 'secret ingredient' like honey, sugar, custard powder, blue cheese, tinned catfood or Bovril. Try them all – and more besides, and good luck to you. Personally, I don't bother much with such alchemy, and I usually manage a reasonable share of carp each season, just by using good uncomplicated bread on its own!

If potatoes are known to catch carp on your own favourite water, the easiest way to get a supply is to buy the small tinned ones; they're about the right size and don't need any cooking. If the Fanny Craddock in you moves you to cook your own however, choose some about one inch long and parboil them, until they're cooked but still reasonably firm, so that they won't crumble when they're put on the hook. They should always by attached with a 'baiting needle', a large-eyed needle through which your reel line is threaded. The threaded needle is then pushed gently through the potato until it emerges from the bottom. The next stage is to slide the potato carefully up the line and tie an eyed hook on. Finally, pull the line and hook into the bait until it is firmly embedded – with not a trace of hook showing. With this method, it will be necessary to re-tie the hook every time the bait is changed; but it's worth it, this bait is an excellent one and is used by many top carp men.

Another very good bait in some lakes is the swan mussel, but take a tip from me and keep them out of the water until they're really 'smelly' before you use them. For some odd reason, they are much more attractive to carp (and tench) when they're like that. To get a supply of swan mussels, use a long rake and search the muddiest, most weedy edges of the lake. You won't ever get large numbers but on the other hand, one good-sized mussel will provide about three or four good-sized baits. Some experts say that certain parts of the mussel only should be used, but I've always used the whole lot – and had plenty of carp and tench to show for it.

Groundbaits for carp should be lightly, nicely done and, if you are bottom fishing, all that's needed is a few morsels of the hook bait, scattered in a narrow circle where you intend to fish. To prove yourself as cunning as the carp, only groundbait with *smaller* versions of the hookbait; breadpaste, cheese, worms, potatoes, mussel or whatever, and do it discreetly, no heavy tramping around the bankside and as little splash as possible when the stuff hits the water. For what it's worth, I rarely groundbait at all for carp, except crucians, and for those chubby little chaps you can 'scale down' most of the hookbaits I've recommended for larger carp. In order of effectiveness, I've found the best crucian hookbaits to be breadcrust (small pieces), breadpaste, maggots and very small worms. For groundbait, simply use occasional offerings of the hookbait, although on some waters, a good milky 'cloud' will often bring a shoal of crucians around.

Tackle: carp tackle can really be divided into two distinct categories: for small carp and for big carp. I say this at the risk of over-simplifying, because, in the majority of carp waters, there's a fair mixture of all sizes. It is possible, however – particularly if you are 'stalking' carp of under six pounds which can be clearly seen in the swim or on the surface – to go for individual fish, without serious risk of hooking a large one. This method also applies to crucians, and for these and other carp within the $\frac{1}{2}$ lb. to 5 lb. range, your heaviest roach rod and fixed spool reel will do. Lines can be around 3 lb. to 4 lb. strain, and hooks no larger than size 10 should be used.

Some crucians can be very shy however, and where you know that these fish only run to a maximum of about 2 lb., your very finest roach tackle can be used. If you know there's a chance of very big crucians, step up the tackle accordingly, as these fish often have a habit of diving into thick weedbeds when hooked.

There's no practical dividing line between these two categories of carp, so now we must seriously look at the best tackle for the large ones. During the 1950s a new rod was pioneered and designed specially for catching big carp by Richard Walker of Hitchin, who found the average 'general' coarse float rod inadequate for controlling carp of over 20 lb. in heavily weeded waters. Originally, this rod was made from split-cane, in two joints with an overall length of 10 ft. It had a full, powerful action, right down to the cork handle, and with it, he caught the present record 44 lb. carp, in a difficult swim – in the dark!

Several more modern versions of this carp rod are available, but usually in hollow fibreglass, with 'spigotted' joints, a 26 in. cork handle and ten or more full-open bridge rings. Another popular feature of these rods is a large butt ring over 1 in. in diameter, and a lined top ring. Quite naturally, the cost of such a rod is appreciably more than for an average roach rod, but once you have one, you'll find it extremely useful for other coarse fish like larger tench, chub and barbel. If you seriously intend to take up specimen carp hunting, early in your angling career, then a good carp rod, as described, would be a good investment. You have to outweigh its greater cost against the fact that it will serve for both float fishing and legering. On the debit side though, successful carping will require certain other items of specialised tackle, which I'll talk about now.

Although the average roach-sized fixed spool reel can be used for carp fishing, particularly crucians and other smaller carp, the 'specimen hunter' should consider something a little larger and more substantial. Most of the top tackle manufacturers make a wide range of reels, and for big carp you should look for one with a spool capacity of at least 200 yds of 8 lb. nylon line, an efficient 'slipping clutch' and, for preference, roller type bearings. Again, this reel could double for other types of fishing; barbel, big chub and tench – even salmon, light sea spinning and bait-fishing, etc. With all tackle, it will pay to have a spare in case of sudden loss or breakage, and although it means digging even deeper into the pocket, you should consider this very seriously.

Lines for carp will depend, to a great extent, on the type of water you are fishing, and the range could be as wide as from 4 lb. to 15 lb. As a general rule, the heavier the carp and weed growth, the stronger the line. Where large carp are hunted in very open, snag-free water, a line of 5 lb. to 6 lb. could be adequate, and will even manage to land fish of 15 lb. to 20 lb.

In dense weed however, you might be 'broken' by comparatively small carp in the 4 lb. to 5 lb. range when using a line of 8 lb. or 9 lb. So, where lines are concerned, be sure to match the strength to the prevailing conditions and remember the notes about lines in the roach section – choose good, smooth, fresh line every time. As with reels, always carry a spare spool of nylon line in your bag; you could be 'broken up' one day to the extent of some 100 yards of line – and 30 miles from the nearest tackle shop!

Hooks: the keen carp fisherman will lavish as much care and attention on his hooks, as a skilled surgeon will on his instruments. As for sizes, this again depends on the size of carp you're fishing for and also the size of bait you're using. In some waters, carp do fall for a couple of maggots, float-fished on a no. 12 hook, but for large balls of breadpaste (which can often be as big as a golf ball) a size 2 hook will not be too large. When you've had a little practice with casting a large bait over long distances, you'll find, very soon, that a large hook will hold the bait much better. In comparison with other coarse fish, carp are extremely cautious, particularly on waters that are heavily fished, so when baiting your hook, always hide every bit of the hook in the bait.

Probably the best type of hooks for carp fishing are the round bend, forged spade-end or eyed variety, and they should always be kept needle sharp, as carp are often struck at long distances and the hook must penetrate, through the bait, into the fish's mouth, with the minimum of delay. Don't ever buy cheap hooks, and even with the more expensive brands, a little attention to the points with a small sharpening stone will not come amiss. Hooks should always be stored and carried in a tin or wallet lined with plastic foam, or similar material, to prevent them rubbing together in transit. They should *never* be returned to the container wet, as even a tiny amount of rust will blunt the points in no time and could even weaken the bend or shanks. I always buy fresh carp hooks every season, just to be on the safe side, and I suggest you do the same.

Float fishing for carp is a method that's fast declining in fashion, as it isn't as convenient or generally successful in comparison with legering and surface fishing. If you like to watch a float however, and I must confess I do on occasions, your tiniest roach float will do for crucians, and something a little bigger for larger carp, small quills with a cork body are ideal. You've probably realised by now that there are few hard and fast rules to coarse fishing, so the question of floats, like other tackle, will be a matter for prevailing conditions. For example, in very deep water, a sliding float might be needed, while in unusually windy weather, a much heavier type of float, similar to that used in long-trotting fast rivers would be a sensible idea. To obtain the maximum pleasure and sport from your fishing, all your tackle, for any type of fish, should be as light as conditions will allow; in this way, the fish stands at least an even chance, and you have the satisfaction of landing him under the most sporting circumstances.

When legering for carp, using a large ball of breadpaste or a small potato, no additional weight will be required on the line. These large baits supply plenty of weight for casting even long distances, and the method is called 'free-lining'. Where weight is necessary, an Arlesey bomb of the appropriate size should be used, or even a small drilled 'bullet'.

Since most carp fishing is carried out with leger tackle, the bite indicator is an extremely important piece of equipment, and over the years, some very novel and clever types have been invented. One of these is the electric type, which is linked to the line between the reel and butt ring, and flashes a light or buzzes (or both) when a fish takes the bait. Other good indicators are more simple and less expensive, including the well tried and tested 'silver paper'. To fish this method, simply take a piece of kitchen foil about 6 in. square and fold it into a slip roughly 4 in. long by $\frac{1}{2}$ in. wide. After casting out the leger tackle, take a loop of loose line down from reel, almost to ground level, then fold your foil 'slip' over once and rest it on the line. Bites are indicated by the foil jumping up towards the butt ring. In windy weather, the whole thing (line and foil) can rest inside a plastic bucket, safe from the breeze. At night, a small shaded torch can be trained on the foil. With this type of indicator, the bale arm of the reel must be *open* all the time.

When you visit your tackle shop, you'll probably see at least one very large landing net on display, a huge thing with strong aluminium or laminated wood arms of up to 48 in. long. The handle will often be telescopic, with a locking device, and the net-mesh will be large. This is a carp net, specially designed for the job, and where these fish run over 20 lb., could mean the difference between success and failure. If you can afford it, buy one – or save for it. Otherwise, get the very largest landing net you can afford. This also applies to keepnets, although my own favourite gimmick is to keep captured carp in a large sack, well out of the sun and in water as deep as possible. In general, I only keep carp for photographing after taking one during a night-fishing session; otherwise, they are returned to the water immediately after weighing.

One other useful 'tool' for the carp men is a pair of artery forceps, which are now available in most good tackle shops. Carp have very leathery mouths, and after being used to dealing with soft-mouthed, soft-lipped fish like roach, you'll have a real surprise when you come to unhook your first carp. These special forceps will grip the hook in locking jaws, allowing steady pressure to be applied to its removal, causing the fish as little discomfort as possible.

Finally, a word about night-fishing gear. Don't worry about the actual method of fishing at night as this will be fully described in the next section. Although carp feed well during the hours of darkness and are frequently caught by anglers at that time, they don't like lights – so make sure your torch or lamp is well shaded, and avoid flashing the beam on the water. Also, it will pay you to paint bait tins, net handles and other 'loose' tackle items white, for easy recognition in the dark. Be *tidy* when fishing at night; gather everything around you, where it can be reached easily and quickly, and don't wander around the waterside unnecessarily, unless you know every inch of bankside, or the moon is exceptionally bright.

Remember also that summer and autumn nights can be very cold, so wear warm clothing, topped with a good nylon wind-cheater. If you're wearing wellington boots, improve the insulation by inserting a pair of special felt 'foot-muffs' to keep out the cold. Even at night, carp are never caught one after the other, and even on the most productive waters, you should be prepared to spend hours at a time, sitting, watching and waiting. That's why your chair, or fishing seat, should be as comfortable as possible, and fitted with a soft canvas back and covered arms, for preference. Your rod-rests should be placed near the seat, ready for a quick strike, and these important items should be of the 'drop line' type with a built-in 'loop' under the rod. This prevents the line from being trapped between the rod and rest, causing unwelcome resistance when a fish takes the bait.

Methods: we have already established that, for fishing purposes, carp can be divided into the small and larger types. Since the smaller carp can be caught by most of the light 'roach' methods, I'll move on right away to the rod-benders, pausing, at the end of the section, for a short passage on how to catch crucian carp – a species for which I have a very special regard.

Now, we'll have to sub-divide again, for big carp fishing consists of three main methods, float fishing, legering or free-lining, and surface fishing. Apart from those who love a float to watch, float fishing is a superior method in very small or very weedy waters, where long-distance casting is unnecessary, or where the weed is so dense that a legered bait would sink into it and be hidden from the fish. In such places, the carp will be shy, especially if they're fished for regularly, so your float must look as 'natural' as possible in the water. I use small floats for this purpose, made from pieces of natural reed, well dried, varnished and fitted with two dark brown rubber float caps. Lengths of peacock quill can also be used in 'quieter' water, and they are very sensitive.

Where thick weed grows to within a foot or so of the surface, a good bait is 'balanced' breadcrust and breadpaste. Simply mould a piece of soft paste around the shank of the hook, then attach a knob of newish crust to the point and barb. When cast, this bait sinks very slowly, just coming to rest on top of the weed. If maggots are used, they have enough buoyancy and lack of weight to settle in the same way. Lobworms and heavier breadpaste, potatoes, etc. are a different proposition and should be fished just on the weed, or slightly above it, by very careful plumbing of the depth and fine adjustment to the float setting. One good alternative method is to fix a small cork ball, or cube, to the line, not far from the hook. Properly adjusted, this should have the effect of 'suspending' the bait over the weeds. While we're on the subject of heavy weed, remember to adjust your line strength accordingly; a big carp 'gone to bed' in a tangled mass of weed or waterlilies really needs some shifting – and it won't be achieved with a line like a spider's web!

For deep water (over one rod-length in depth) a sliding float will be necessary, and the principle of this has already been covered in the tackle section. In windy weather, try an antenna float, or one with a low centre of gravity, but remember that if a baited tackle is 'floating in the waves' it might present a very unnatural appearance to the fish. On reasonably weed-free stillwaters and rivers of moderate flow, the 'laying-on' method of float fishing can be used, and this rig is best made up of a peacock quill float of about 4 in. in length, with a small bored bullet stopped at the bottom end with a split-shot, all finished off with a nice sharp hook – the size of which will depend on the type of bait being used. As a general coarse fishing method, for roach, tench, chub, bream and larger dace and rudd, it is probably the most successful and sensitive ever devised.

Legering with weighted tackle, that is with a bullet or lead bomb, should only be used when the weight is essential for long casting; otherwise, the 'freelining' technique, with nothing on the line but the hook and bait, is easily the most sensitive rig. Once you have played a carp on unweighted tackle, you will know the difference, for even the smallest bomb or bullet 'dampens' the action of the fish – and is also inclined to snag in weed and other obstructions. All the aforementioned baits may be used for legering, including the balanced paste/crust for weedy water, but in most carp fisheries, the ball of breadpaste or small potato will usually take the better fish.

If a weight must be used, it should always be allowed to run *up* the line when a fish moves away with the bait, in other words, the split-shot comes below the weight, never above. Ground-baiting is rarely necessary when legering, particularly long-range legering. If you are using the leger in a pool very close to the bank, a few samples of hookbait might help, otherwise forget it. One other exception could be where carp, in a particular water, are being weaned on a new bait, potato for example. In cases like this, a few small potatoes, thrown into the anticipated swims, will help to educate the carp.

In recent years, surface fishing has accounted for many large carp, and it is a method I'm very fond of. Like fly-fishing for trout, your fish must be 'stalked' and located, then a surface bait is drifted or cast (very gently) nearby. The floating bread-crust is easily the most successful of these baits, and for sheer excitement, the approach of a large visible carp, with rubbery lips already parted to mouth the breadcrust, has little equal among any other types of coarse fishing. Many novice carp anglers have great difficulty in casting breadcrust on a weight-less line, and in my experience this is usually because they are using pieces too small to provide enough weight. If you know your carp run between six and thirty pounds, don't be afraid to use crusts of anything from $1\frac{1}{2}$ in. to 3 in. square, and if this size of bait is briefly dipped in the water before casting, you'll find that it has ample weight to get out a fair distance. If you still have trouble and there is some wind about, use this as an ally and 'drift' the bait out to the fish. It takes a little longer, but presents the crust in a very natural fashion.

Another golden rule for surface-fishers: keep your reel in tip-top condition, always. Fill the spool with line right to the lip, and keep the works well oiled. Any reputable reel, furnished as I've described, should still cast good distances, even with little weight to help. As many carp waters support hoards of 'small fry' like tiny roach, rudd, etc., you might get some unwelcome attention to your floating crust. This bait, however large, seems to attract fry like a magnet. In normal circumstances, this will not matter, and I'm sure that if anything, the movement of small fish near the crust helps to draw big carp to the spot. If this small fry activity becomes too violent, however, you must use a larger piece of bread to compensate for what the little raiders are eating.

I suppose at least half of my own big carp were taken on the floating breadcrust, but at certain times I have experienced what the trout fly fisherman would call a 'short take', This is when the carp noses the crust, perhaps even pushes it along the surface a few inches, then swims away without taking it. When this happens, try reducing the size of the bait considerably, even in spite of the small fry activity, or alternatively, nip on a small split-shot, about 2 in, from the hook until the bait is *just* submerged. Both these tricks can induce shy carp to a much more 'positive' take on occasions.

A word about striking bites on floating baits. Apart from the 'short takers' I have described, a good-sized carp will leave you in little doubt that he has the bait. Usually, he will nose around for a while and even mouth the bait, but once he makes up his mind, he'll take the bull by the horns, engulfing the crust in his big lips and turning down into the water – even flipping his tail on the surface as he goes This is one of the most exciting moments I know in coarse fishing, and when it happens to you for the first time, don't panic, keep calm (if you can) and give the fish about four seconds, from the time of taking, before you strike. The strike itself should be a firm, half upwards, half sideways (opposite direction to the fish) sweep of rod. Now, he should be on! And I'll be explaining how to play big carp at the end of this section . . .

When the wind drift is exceptionally heavy, an 'anchored' floating crust can be fished. With this method, simply attach an Arlesey bomb or bored bullet, of the appropriate size, to the line, about twice the depth of the water away from the hook. A heavier strike will be necessary, to take up the angle between the weight and bait. This weight should always be allowed to run up the line, being stopped off with a firmly closed split-shot *below* the weight.

If purely floating baits are used on a free line, you might find the surface scum on the water has a tendency to sink the line, after a few hours fishing. To counteract this, apply some line 'floatant' which most tackle shops sell, usually for dry-fly fishermen.

In rivers and other flowing waters, surface baits can be used, probably drifted downstream, almost like 'trotting the stream' without a float, and the best places to try, particularly on heavily-fished waters, are under bushes or overhanging trees against the opposite bank. I've had some good carp on this tackle, fishing the river Brue at Basin Bridge in Somerset.

Night fishing for carp has increased in popularity ever since the record 44 pounder was taken in darkness, but if you're keen to try it, be sure to explore the water thoroughly beforehand. Decide on a particular swim, and 'map out' all the more obvious snags and inshore obstructions. On moonless nights, muddy water tends to merge with the bankside, and a foot in the wrong place could spell disaster. Never fish alone at night, the successful landing of a big carp in these conditions is definitely a two-man job; one with the rod, the other wielding the landing net; and if you or your companion are ever tempted to 'go into the water' to net a difficult fish, my advice is *don't* – that sort of caper can be dangerous enough in daylight, especially where very muddy, weedy lakes are concerned. Last, but not least, always ensure that night fishing is allowed on your water – some clubs and private owners won't permit it, for obvious reasons.

Once you have hooked a big carp, you'll need all the skill and determination that you can muster to bring it to the net. In most cases, your carp will make a first headlong rush, once he feels the hook, sometimes taking as much as fifty yards or more of line. Don't try to stop him at this stage, unless he has been hooked very near to thick weeds or similar obstructions, in which case, steady 'sidestrain' should be applied, to turn his head into some more open water. Otherwise, let him run, keeping a firm pressure on the line by holding the rod at an angle of roughly 30°, letting him bend the rod down to the corks if he's a very big one. Never reel in against a running fish when using the fixed spool reel; it is not only dangerous, but will also put kinks in the line. The correct way is to wait until the fish has stopped, then 'pump' him by sweeping the rod upwards to take up some slack and reeling it back as you go. The general rule when playing a big carp – and this will apply to other large coarse fish – is to keep a tight line, but not too tight, right up to the time of netting. The only exception would be if a fish gets bedded down in thick weeds or roots and no amount of pumping or pressure will release him. In cases like this, the line should be slackened considerably for several minutes if necessary. If you're lucky, a fish will sometimes find his own way out of the snag without breaking your tackle.

Never be in a big hurry to bring your carp ashore; having waited hours on end for a bite, don't ruin the whole thing by rushing the landing, but be sure the fish is thoroughly tired first. Usually, the time is right when the carp is wallowing on his side, close to your bank, but even so, be careful – these big fish have a habit of coming to life at the last moment, and a final surge, on a short, tight line usually ends only one way.

Landing should be carried out by two anglers, as I've already suggested. Just before the carp is finally beaten and is being drawn slowly inshore for netting, your companion should lower the net gently into the water, keeping a very firm grasp on the handle. The fish must then be brought over the rim of the net, and the 'netter' makes a firm upward sweep, at the same time walking quickly backwards, grasping the net above the fish and below the rim, to trap him in the mesh. Always get the fish well up the bank, particularly if it is a sloping bank. There's nothing more frustrating than a good carp jumping from the net, back into the water. Big fish should always be weighed *in the net*, or a suitable separate string bag. Finally, always return your carp to the water, as soon as possible – and never take fish away, unless it's so large you're going to put it in a glass case.

Now, a few words about crucian carp. Unlike bigger carp, crucians are shoal fish, so once you catch one, there should be more to follow. Because of this, a light groundbait should be used, a little at a time, to keep them interested, and a good, finely-mashed bread mixture, laced with a few maggots (if you're using them on the hook) can be used. Crucians have small mouths, so hook size should not exceed no. 12 unless you know you're on a specimen crucian water, where fish in the 3 lb. to 4 lb. class can be expected. If this should be the case, hooks of up to no. 8 can be used.

Floats for crucian fishing must be light and very sensitive; crow quills and 1 in. lengths of peacock quill are ideal. These fish register some very odd bites and are sometimes inclined to 'play' with the bait, so don't wait for a firm downward plunge of the float, but strike at almost every little movement. On many occasions, I've lifted my tackle, thinking that the bait had gone, only to hook a crucian – who had been lying there with the bait in his mouth, not moving the float an inch!

Crucians will feed at most water depths, and when a shoal is contacted, it's a question of finding the best depth. Always use a slowly sinking bait, preferably a couple of small maggots or pieces of breadflake or crust about the size of half a fingernail. If your crucians are partial to breadpaste, this can be made to sink more slowly by 'flattening' a small ball of it into a disc, no more than $\frac{1}{2}$ in. in diameter. Other crucians can be taken on worms and, in my experience, these should be smaller types like marsh or brandling worms. Larger crucian carp are sometimes taken on light leger tackle, but because of their peculiar biting habits, it's not a method I favour. When hooked, the crucian – even a very small one – will amaze you with the swift, darting fight, but continual activity in a crucian swim doesn't seem to bother the fish unduly, and once you have them 'on the boil', catches of twenty or thirty fish can be made, on many waters.

CHAPTER 6

Tench

The very thought of them, tench, those silky-smooth, muscular fighters of the high summer; yes, I must confess, right away and without apology – they're my very favourite of all the coarse fish. The ideal tench water, too, has often been painted in words by the more poetic of our angling writers, and generally speaking, I'll go along with most of them. Imagine a beautiful private manor house lake of about ten acres, fringed with tall shady trees and edged with thick flowering waterlilies; pigeons coo, moorhens cluck and bees drone in the early morning sunshine. Well, some years ago that scene would have been typical, but since then, many clubs and other angling bodies have discovered the pure joy of these handsome fighting tench for themselves, and once barren gravel pits, sluggish canals which only held small rudd and spiny sticklebacks, and many other much less exclusive waters have now been stocked with tench, which are hardy, adaptable fish and pure delight on the end of the line.

Tench are essentially a fish of the slower rivers, canals and still waters, more particularly in the southern counties where summer arrives a little earlier, places like the Norfolk Broads and rivers, and the rivers and drains of Somerset. The Fenlands of Cambridgeshire, Huntingdon and Lincoln also hold good tench, and in some of the Cheshire meres they run quite large. In the midlands of southern Ireland too, some rivers and lakes produce very good tench, and many of these waters are hardly ever fished. Do not even dismiss any very small farm ponds that you might know; it's surprising how many tiny waters like these hold a good head of tench, and although they will probably be small ones, they can give the beginner some excellent sport and practice.

Normally, you'll see little signs of tench before April, as they tend to bury themselves in the mud during the hard winter months, but when the weather warms up and the first cuckoo is heard, they'll start to move into the shallows – where they can often be seen, if you keep still and quiet. Later, around mid-May or early June, they will start feeding in earnest, churning up the mud on the bottom and producing strings of 'needle' bubbles on the surface. This is how they can best be detected, but be careful, crucian carp can make similar bubblings.

Like bream, tench will shoal in large numbers and, once you've found a feeding shoal and providing you fish for them in the right way, it will be possible to catch quite a few at a sitting. At any time between the end of April and the beginning of August (according to the weather) the tench will begin spawning, and if you hide yourself at the side of the lake near to shallow, weedy water that's fairly clear, you'll witness a sight to fill you with wonder – scores of tench in pairs, dashing and 'porpoising' in and out of the weeds, literally pushing each other around in an exciting reproductive ritual. When it's all over, they tend to go off the feed for several weeks and will seldom reach the same degree of hunger they had in early June. No, you'll have to wait another whole year for that fabulous early-season bonanza.

Baits: for tench, baits are usually simple and uncomplicated; breadcrust, breadpaste, maggots and small worms – and that's it, apart from the more obvious 'swan mussel' waters which I told you about in the chapter on carp. Very often, it will pay you to fish a slowly sinking bait for tench; a small piece of bread-crust, a trio of maggots or a small red worm will all sink slowly to the bottom, providing your weight is not too near the hook. Tench will sometimes feed quite close to the surface and when they do, a slowly sinking morsel seems quite natural to them. Other good tench baits include soft cheese paste, lobworms and swan mussels. Occasionally, baits like tinned catfood and luncheon meat will take them, so my advice is – experiment with your tench baits, especially when they get fussy towards the end of July. I know one angler who used to get bags of tench from the club lake time after time, when everyone else had two or three at the most. In an off-guard moment I wrung his secret from him. Know what it was ? Would you believe, bits of banana!

Goundbaits for tench. In spite of my slow-sinking bait method, most of your tench will be caught on the bottom, probably using the 'lift' method as described for roach. For all bottom fishing, groundbait will be required and all types of bread, bran and meal will do; but don't overdo it, a bucketful for an average day's fishing should be more than enough in most still waters – and don't forget to include some of the hookbait. When he mixes groundbait for tench, Alan Vare gets hold of some fresh ox blood. He swears by this, although I don't know exactly where he gets it.

Where the bottom of your tench water is not too thick with black mud, but contains some loose gravel or other hard matter, raking the swim you're going to fish can help a lot, particulatly in June when the coarse fishing season begins. It has the effect of stirring up the minute organisms and food particles upon which the tench feed and will hold the fish in a swim for quite a while. The right type of rake is described in the 'tackle' section of this chapter, and it's always a good idea to rake your swim the night before fishing, providing you don't live too far from the water. When you have finished raking, dump in some groundbait, and the following morning on arrival, rake it again – lightly this time, then put in more groundbait.

By the time it's all settled, your tackle should be made up and the tench all ready and waiting. One would think that all that raking and disturbance would frighten the tench away, but in all of the waters I fish – and rake – this isn't so. Within 10 minutes of raking, you'll probably spot those needle bubbles, indicating a shoal of hungry tench after the rakings and ground-bait. An exciting moment, that.

Tackle: at the risk of upsetting the leger men, I'm going to recommend float fishing for tench, every time. I know it might sound a little old-fashioned to some of the specimen-hunting types, especially those who cast out huge lumps of swan mussel on weightless legers, and haul in 6½ lb. tench every so often. For me, the whole flavour of tench fishing is a small white float, mirrored in the calm green water of a secluded lake, with the first flush of dawn light glowing through the trees. This is essentially a beginner's book, and unless my reader gleans at least a good degree of 'atmosphere' when he reads these lines – and when he goes fishing – I'm sure he'll miss a lot.

For general float fishing, your hollow glass match rod will be ideal and will afford you fine sport as it throbs with life, cushioning the powerful shocks and plunges of a fighting tench. For legering, if you must, your roach leger rod will do. In the same way, the fixed spool reel you bought for roach will be adequate for tench, but be sure it has a really good slipping clutch, as big tench will often rip quite a few yards of line from the reel in his first rush. Lines for tench will vary according to the water conditions, but in open, almost weedless water, lines as light as 2 lb. could be used; they could also be a distinct advantage, where the fish are very shy biters. I fish several such waters and find my entire roach outfit quite adequate for tench in the 2 lb. to 4 lb. class, but even so, the larger fish do need some delicate handling on these very light lines, consequently, the minimum strength I'd recommend for the beginner is 4 lb. Thickly-weeded tench waters, well sprinkled with fallen trees and other tackle-breaking snags, will require heavier lines, up to 8 lb. would not be too heavy, even though the fish only run to 4 lb. at the largest.

Hook sizes will be governed by bait size, but in general, sizes 14 to 10 will be most appropriate, the larger hooks for baits like big lobworms and balls of breadpaste. In all cases, *strong* hooks are essential, and the forged type should be used. The choice of eyed or spade-end will be up to you, but for what it's worth, I normally use eyed hooks for large baits and spade-ends for the smaller ones.

Floats should be small and sensitive, preferably with a bright 'dayglo' painted tip to show up against dark water, particularly in the early morning and late evening hours. The ideal float is a 2 in. to 6 in. length of peacock quill, the longer length being used in deeper water. This float is the perfect companion to the 'lift' method of bottom fishing, which I described in detail in the section on roach. Heavier floats or antenna floats could be needed when conditions are unusually windy, or for fishing at long range, but in general, keep to the smaller floats wherever it is possible.

Other items of tackle like shot, weights, disgorger or forceps, landing net and rod-rests you already have, as you bought them for roach fishing. The only additional item the tench angler will need is a swim 'rake' which can easily be made by joining two ordinary garden rake heads together 'back to back' with the prongs facing outwards. Tie these together firmly with strong plastic-covered wire or nylon rope. Through the 'eyes' on the rake-heads attach a length of strong nylon rope, with a wrist loop at the end for holding on to. When in use, the rake should be cast out, then drawn slowly through the swim, avoiding thick lily roots and very heavy fallen branches, etc. All rubbish raked in should be stacked well away from the waterside, preferably hidden by bushes, etc.

Methods: for general tench fishing, the two most efficient methods are the 'lift' method and 'laying-on' or float legering, as fully described in the roach section. Other floats and rigs can be used, according to water conditions, and these include straightforward legering and the slowly sinking bait, where the weight must be close under the float.

When you hook your first tench – and what a thrill that's going to be! – you'll probably be surprised by its sheer strength and dogged fighting ability, so don't be caught off guard, even if your rod is bending right down to the handle; keep your head, hang on and show him who's the boss! If he wants to run, let him, but normally, he won't run very far, nevertheless, steer

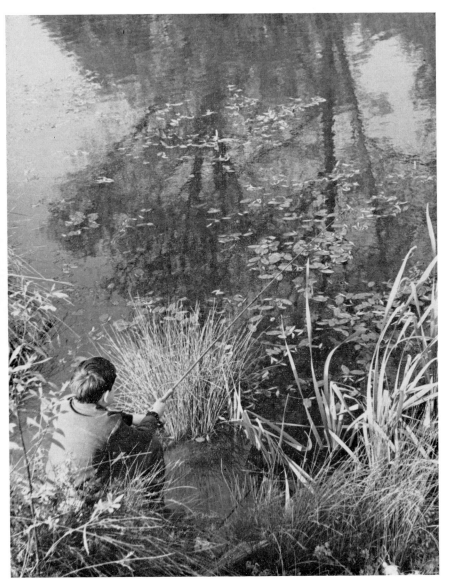

Pleasant fishing in a weedy gravel pit

Roach . . .

. . . and Rudd

Bronze (Common) Bream

(*top*) Common Carp (*centre*) Crucian Carp, (*bottom left*) Mirror Carp (*bottom right*) Leather Carp

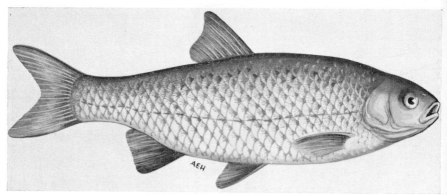

Chub

Perch

Barbel

Dace

Tench

Coarse Fishing Tackle. (1) Landing Net (2) Rod Holdall (3) Match Rod (4) Carp Rod (5) Leger/Spinning Rod (6) Multiplier Reel (7) Fixed Spool Reel (8) Electric Bite Indicator (9) Centrepin Reel (10) Semi Closed Face Reel (11) Rod Rests (12) Gaff

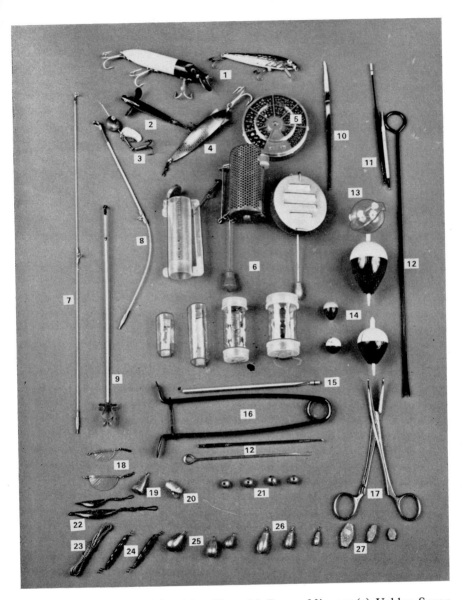

Coarse Fishing Tackle. (1) Diving Plugs (2) Devon Minnow (3) Voblex Spoon (4) Toby Lure (5) Split Shot Dispenser (6) Swim Feeders and Bait Droppers (7) Quivertip (8) Swingtip (9) Butt Indicator (10) Porcupine Quill Float (11) Match Floats (12) Disgorger (13) Bubble Float (14) Pike Floats (15) Tube Disgorger (16) Pike Gag (17) Forceps (18) Anti-kink Vane (19) Plummet (20) Spring Plummet (21) Drilled Bullets (22) Anti-kink Leads (23) Lead Wire (24) Spiral Leads (25) Wye Leads (26) Arlesey Bombs (27) Coffin Leads

(*top*) the Throop Fishery, River Stour, Dorset. (*centre*) the Great Ouse at Godman-chester. (*bottom*) an 11 lb. river pike

him clear of thick weeds and other obstructions by applying steady side pressure – within the limits of your tackle, of course. Gradually, he should be reduced to a slow circling around the swim, with an occasional deep plunge, so keep a firm rein on him until he's close in to the side of the bank, rolling over on his flank, beaten. Just before he's brought close inshore, sink the landing net in the water, or better still, get your companion to do it, then draw your tench over the net gently and lift him out. Be very careful though, many tench make a last desperate dash when they see the net, so be ready to give him line.

The second pleasant surprise in store for you is the sheer beauty of the tench. He'll be silky-smooth to the touch, olive green in colour – even a dark golden shade on some waters – and you'll be impressed by the muscular shoulders and big, powerful tail. Such a lovely, spirited creature deserves not only your admiration, but your compassion as well, so please – return him to the water right away.

CHAPTER 7

Chub

Picture a fast, crystal clear river, set in a green country meadow, with an occasional wide bend, perhaps a sparkling weirpool and, for preference, a generous sprinkling of overhanging trees and bushes. Chub! Yes, this fine fish is a creature of the running waters: he's elusive, shy, difficult to locate and not at all easy to catch. But once you've hooked him, watch out! He's a fast, strong fighter, particularly in his first rush, and is a wizard at finding ways to break your tackle; roots, rocks, weeds, anchor chains – he knows his home territory well.

Although it's true to say that a few chub have settled happily in lakes and other still waters, he must be generally thought of as a river fish. Many rivers and streams throughout the country have chub, and they can also be found in a few Scottish rivers, like the Annan, for example. I don't know of any in Ireland, but I'm sure he will reach the Emerald Isle some day. Notable chub rivers include the Hampshire Avon, the Great Ouse, Dorset Stour, Thames, Swale, Severn, Kennet, parts of the Lea and many more rivers and streams throughout the south and north.

When going after chub, don't restrict yourself to the big rivers; some very large fish are to be taken from backwaters and sidestreams, especially after a heavy flood has turned the main river into a thick, raging torrent. As for locating chub, the password should always be 'softly, softly' for if you stamp and shout around the riverbank, or flash bright clothing, your chub will quietly *sink* from sight, like a dim shadow. But if you're careful and hide yourself in some good cover like thick reeds or bankside bushes, you may watch the chub gliding around or taking flies and other insects from the surface.

Baits: providing they are in a feeding mood, chub will gobble up almost anything you throw at them; maggots, breadcrust or paste, cheese, all kinds of worms, luncheon meat, tinned cat-food, sausage meat, slugs, beetles, caterpillars, frogs, flies, minnows and other small fish – the list is almost endless.

In recent years, small crayfish have accounted for some very big chub, particularly on the upper Great Ouse; but this being a rather specialised, specimen hunter's method, I'd recommend you to use, and get used to, the more conventional baits first. In my own experience, cheese paste, breadcrust and worms – in that order – have proved to be the best all-round baits, but I'm always experimenting and I suggest that you do the same.

Groundbaiting for chub should always consist of samples of the hookbait, smaller pieces for preference, so that your bait becomes the largest and most attractive morsel being offered. In very fast rivers however, the groundbait *must* come to rest near your bait, and not get carried off downstream, taking the chub away with it. This can be achieved by making a heavier groundbait mix like the one already described for roach; cricket-ball-sized lumps of mashed bread and meal enclosed around a few pebbles to get it to the bottom quickly. This stuff must always be made up with the absolute minimum of water, otherwise it will invariably break up when it hits the surface. Another method of introducing groundbait is the open-end swimfeeder, but more about that in the nest section.

Tackle: this will usually depend upon the size of chub you are going after, and I should have mentioned something about chub weights at the beginning of the chapter. A good average size would be about 1 lb., but on many streams the average could be much lower. 3 lb. to 4 lb. chub are specimens in my book, although fish over 8 lb. have been recorded, and six pounders are not uncommon from the Royalty fishery on the

Hampshire Avon. The smaller chub are often taken when roach fishing, and if I were you, I'd concentrate on these, just to get your hand in.

If you're float fishing, your roach tackle will do, although it will be necessary to step up line strength and hook size a little. It really is a question of bait too: if a single maggot is being used, the hook could be from size 14 to 12, but larger baits like cheese and bread paste, worms and meat baits, a no. 8 to 4 wouldn't be too large. Some people fish the crayfish for chub (usually for the four to seven pounders), and a hook size up to no. 1 is the tool for this job.

For general, everyday chubbing however, trotting the stream with 'stepped up' roach tackle will be quite good enough, and single maggot bait apart, remember that of all the coarse fish, with the exception of pike, chub have the largest mouths, so be generous with bait sizes; use cheese and breadpaste balls at least $\frac{1}{2}$ in. in diameter, preferably much larger, and where worms are concerned, I've found even average-sized chub partial to them presented in bunches of three or four!

Legering can also take good chub, and here again, use a heavier version of your roach leger tackle, although the same rod will do. I've often found the best chub in either weedy, or very snaggy parts of the river, and the best paintings of chub always show them lurking in thick, submerged tree roots. Well, there's a lot of truth in this, so if you intend to use a swimfeeder, be prepared to lose a few before the day is out.

Another good method is livebaiting, as chub can be very keen on minnows and other small fish, if they're presented in the right way. If you refer to the section on perch, it will tell you all you need to know, but be careful, this is really a method for larger chub, and these fish run larger than the largest perch.

Some people spin for chub, and although I've tried this method on several occasions, I've had little success. But don't let my lack of enthusiasm deter you, it can be a very pleasant way to catch them, particularly on a cold winter's day when chub will often 'move' while all the other fish are skulking out of sight. If spinning tickles your fancy, the outfit as described for perch will be more than adequate.

If you want a crack at the chub record, then try fishing a live crayfish for bait. This is considerably heavier than the other recommended baits, and is meant almost exclusively for the bigger fish, so a change of tackle will be necessary. The carp rod (see carp chapter) is the tool for this job, and you'll need a no. 1 hook, with a line of at least 5 lb.

Before I forget, and getting back to trotting the stream with float tackle, a 'centre-pin' reel can be used, as described in the roach chapter. Fished from a boat moored *across* the stream, this can be a delightful way to spend a day's chubbing, the fast current taking the line straight from the reel as the float tackle drifts downstream. Groundbait in the usual 'river' way, and change your bait if the fish don't bite or get finnicky; and don't forget to take your minnow trap along, one of these little fish, presented live at about mid-water could account for the chub of a lifetime. Unless you're already an experienced boat-user however, I'd advise you to take along a more seasoned angler with you, for boats can be tricky methods of transport on fast waters.

Back to crayfish for a moment, this bait can be 'free-lined', which means no weight or lead is used on the line. In any case, a good cray gives plenty of weight, even for long-distance casting, and the lack of anything else on the tackle is a big advantage with shy-biting chub, who are inclined to reject a bait if a lot of resistance is felt.

Methods: well, these seem to have been adequately covered in the chub tackle section, and the long-trotting with float tackle, legering with general baits and live or dead fish, freelining (not only crayfish but other baits too), livebaiting and spinning; all are excellent methods for chub, in winter or summer.

Generally, the bite of a chub, whether on float or leger tackle, will be quite bold; the float will plunge under quickly, or the leger bite indicator (whichever one you're using) will leave you in no doubt that something has hit the bait. If anything, you should strike fairly quickly with chub, as delay can cause the

85

fish to take the hook well down in the mouth. Chub have some very formidable 'throat' teeth, and even if you use artery forceps to extract the hook, they can inflict nasty wounds on your fingers – so watch out!

If you find chub in still waters, the only method that you can't use is trotting the stream.

CHAPTER 8

Pike

Rivers, streams, lakes, ponds, reservoirs, canals and pits will all hold pike, large or small; they're creatures of all waters and places, from tiny, south-country farm ponds to the majestic, fast-flowing salmon rivers of northern Scotland. Wherever there are quantities of small fish to be chased and devoured, you'll find the 'river tiger' lurking under the weeds, behind rocks and stones, and even beneath anchored boats.

Generally speaking, the largest pike seem to come from big lakes and reservoirs and this is probably due to the fact that, in still water, he has no strong current to combat, consequently, will put on more weight because he's using less energy to seek his prey. In Britain, you shouldn't have far to travel for some pike fishing, and as for locating them, simply watch the surface of the water where shoals of small roach, dace, bleak or rudd are sporting themselves. Pretty soon, if pike are about, the little fish will scatter in alarm as one rushes through the swim, slashing and gulping as he goes, even turning back on his tail to devour any poor little tiddler he might have injured in his first attack.

In some of the deeper lakes and reservoirs where pike run to 30 lb. or more, very little surface activity will be seen. These huge fish tend to lurk in the depths, only moving occasionally to take a good-sized mouthful at a time – and this could mean fish of over three pounds in weight – including his own kind!

Some of the better-known pike waters include Slapton Ley in

Devon, the Norfolk Broads and rivers, particularly Hickling Broad and Heigham Sound; several of the London reservoirs, the river Wye in Wales, the Fen rivers and drains, and of course, the big lakes and rivers of Ireland. A pike of two pounds will give a good account of himself on light tackle; the six-pound-plus fish will need some careful treatment, and anything larger than 15 lb. is a specimen – to be treated with some respect, in the water and out!

Baits: as we will fish for pike almost entirely with small fish baits and artificial 'lures', I'll divide this section into three parts; livebaits deadbaits and lures. The various ways of fishing these follow.

Livebaits. Where pike are to be presented with a natural, moving fish bait, the obvious answer is to use small fish caught from the water your pike are living in. If this is not possible, bait fish can be obtained from other waters, but make sure that it is allowed; some fisheries forbid the removal of fish under any circumstances. Also, other waters will not allow fish from 'foreign' fisheries to be brought in, for fear of over-stocking or possible disease.

Small roach, rudd, dace, bleak, bream, gudgeon and even very small pike are all suitable for livebaiting, and if you can obtain them, try a spritely little goldfish. That's a special little secret of my own! As a general rule, use larger livebaits for larger pike, it's all a matter of proportion. In a pike water where small fish are very numerous, a half-hour session with light roach tackle and a single maggot on the hook should provide enough livebait for an average day's piking. To keep baits lively, which is important, use a keep net with very small 'minnow' size mesh – and keep it immersed in deepish water, well out of the sun. Special livebait 'kettles' are also obtainable. Other baits will catch pike, and these include worms and maggots, but in the main, these will attract the smaller pike, and you could be troubled with perch and eels.

Deadbaits. Many keen pike anglers call in at the wet fish shop for a paperful of fresh sprats or small herrings. These sea fish are rich in oil and when fished on the bottom, make a most attractive bait for big pike. For this type of 'laying-on' or legering, the smaller coarse fish can also be used. Some anglers catch their bait fish well beforehand and preserve them in airtight jars in a solution of formalin (preservative) and water. Although this can be a useful standby when livebaits are difficult to obtain, I've never found them as successful as freshly-caught baits. Formalin has a strong odour, and must be thoroughly washed out of baits before they're used.

Lures. Spinning or plug fishing can be a delightful way to fish for pike, and all that's needed is suitable spinning tackle (see tackle section following) and a haversack with some spinners, plugs, disgorger or pliers, gag and gaff. With such light, portable equipment, the pike man may roam at will, making his casts into all the likely places, covering large expanses of water until he finds a fish, then moving on in search of more. Good spinning lures for pike can be purchased or made, and all these, plus the other items of necessary pike tackle, will now be described in detail.

Tackle: because pike tackle is so specialised, in comparison with that used for other coarse fish, the tackle and fishing methods sections will be combined – to avoid repetition.

A lot of fun can be had by fishing for small pike, say fish up to about 5 lb., with roach tackle, using worms or very small live or dead fish for bait. Take a roach rod, fixed spool reel, 4 lb. line, cork-bodied float and small bored bullet resting on a split shot. Finish it off with an eyed or spade-end hook of about size 8. Your roach landing net, plus a little fine groundbait to attract tiny fish around you, and a suitable disgorger or forceps will complete the rig. Now you're equipped for little pike, but as even these babies have a mouthful of very sharp teeth, they should not be given much time after taking the bait, otherwise the hook will be taken well down into the jaws and the line could be chewed through. The best remedy for this is to attach a 1 ft length of fine 'Elasticum' wire to the hook.

I sometimes amuse myself in this way, but only on one particular water where the pike rarely grow larger than 4 lb., and the average, in fact, is only 2 lb. or so. For the beginner, this style of piking makes an interesting and useful introduction, but I would only recommend it on waters similar to the one that I have just described. To use such fine tackle where 20 lb. pike exist would be courting disaster.

So, having dealt with small pike, let's move on to the big ones. Since the three basic pike fishing methods are livebaiting, deadbaiting and spinning (which includes plug fishing), the tackle will be described separately, under each category.

Livebaiting. The ideal rod for this purpose is the carp rod, and the heavier fixed spool reel that I recommended for carp. A centrepin reel can be used, particularly where long casting is not necessary, and in many ways, is a more efficient and pleasant reel for playing large fish. But whichever reel you use, arm it with at least 100 yards of 12 lb. line – even stronger stuff where very large pike are present. Some of the big, egg-shaped floats sold for livebaiting are, in my view, much too heavy for the purpose and make a terrible splash when they hit the water; they can also cause unnecessary resistance to a taking pike. Well, I'm not suggesting that pike are shy, retiring fish, but I do believe in quiet and stealth whenever possible. Therefore, your float should be as small as possible, according to the weight of the livebait.

In recent years, the conventional rig of huge cork 'bung' with one (or even two) 'pilot' floats has largely been outdated. These pilot floats were used to indicate the direction in which a hooked pike was running, but personally, I never use them, preferring as little weight and obstruction on my line as possible. These days I use a cork float about 2 in. long and $1\frac{1}{4}$ in. in diameter, slotted at the side to take a wooden holding peg. This, and all my other pike floats, is finished with a bright orange 'Dayglo' paint, which shows up extremely well on the water.

Always use a wire 'trace' for pike fishing. These can be bought already made up with hooks and swivels attached, and even fitted with single or treble hooks, You can make them up yourself and it will be cheaper; simply buy a reel of wire of about 10 lb. to 15 lb. strain and preferably nylon-covered to prevent rust. Swivels and hooks are easily attached with pliers, and you can make quite a few spare ones of different sizes at very little cost.

Some pike anglers still use 'snap tackles' which are bought ready made up; they have two or three treble hooks which can be moved along the wire to suit the size of livebait being used, and they also have a loop at the end for attaching to the reel line. Personally, I find them too heavy and old fashioned, as the wire traces are usually made from needlessly thick, twisted wire which often has a tendency to rusting. No, a single treble hook, size 8 to 4, according to the livebait size, mounted on a 2 ft length of plastic-coated wire, will be quite adequate. Swivels are important as they allow the trace to revolve or twist without putting kinks in the reel line. A good, lively livebait can perform all sorts of antics in the water, so look to your swivels, and ideally, put one between to hook and wire, and another where the trace joins the reel line. Some weight will be necessary to 'cock' the float in the water if the bait isn't heavy enough to do the trick, and for this purpose, an ordinary bored bullet, of appropriate size and stopped with a split-shot will do.

When fishing a livebait, the rod can be kept in rests, as you will normally get plenty of warning when a pike takes the bait, but leave the pick-up on the reel open or the pike could smash the line in its first rush. Usually, when a pike takes your bait, the float will first bob under, surface, run along a little, bob under again, then move off, submerging steadily, like a submarine. Once it's completely submerged, count seven, then strike – with a firm upward sweep of the rod. If it's a big one, give him his head, and don't be in a hurry to get him on the bank.

Deadbaiting. This is really a straightforward legering method, and the tackle described for livebaiting will fit the bill, with the exception of the float, which will not be required. Deadbaits can be any bright, silvery coarse fish (avoid the spiny ones) or sprats or herrings from the fishmonger. Using a baiting needle, take your wire trace through the gill-cover of the bait and out again at the 'vent', which is on the underside of the fish, just before the anal fin. Then attach a treble hook, of appropriate size, to the end of the trace. A swivel should be tied where the reel line joins the trace. With medium-to-large deadbaits, no additional casting weight will be necessary, but in waters where pike will only take very small baits, a bomb or bored bullet can be used. Deadbait 'flights' are available from the tackle shop; they have a leaded spike to insert into the bait, plus at least two treble hooks. If you're rich, by all means get some, otherwise make up your own.

Your drop line rod-rests should be used for deadbait legering, also some type of bite indicator. Personally, the only indicator I use is to leave the pick-up off the reel, and when a good pike runs off with the bait, somewhere in the middle of the lake, the line snakes off the reel at a pretty fair rate. Unmistakable!

When casting live or dead baits, reel the baited tackle up to within some 2 ft of the rod-top, then holding the rod at 30°, give an easy up-and-sideways swing out, not forgetting to take your line-retaining finger off the spool at the right moment.

Spinning and Plug Fishing. For lighter spinning, using small lures, the standard leger rod will suffice, but for heavier work with weighted 'spoons' and plugs over 3 in. long, the carp rod should be used. Special spinning rods are available, in a variety of lengths and patterns, but for a start, use the two rods I have suggested. Later, if you become really addicted to pike spinning, or take up light inshore sea fishing, like spinning for bass, then a special spinning rod could be an investment.

If you do take to really serious spinning, your choice of reel will be extremely important, as continual casting and retrieving, without trouble, will be an essential to success. If you have chosen your 'general' coarse fishing reel wisely, however, it should perform as required, but keep it well oiled and free from dirt and grit. The 'multiplier' reel can also be used for spinning; this is basically a centrepin type of reel with an extremely free-running spool, and it is specially geared for a very fast rate of retrieve. Casting from this reel takes a lot of practice, and to save the beginner untold frustration, I'll not recommend it for pike spinning, at this stage.

Lines for spinning will range from 7 lb. for light work to 12 lb. to 16 lb. for heavier spinning with the carp rod. In all cases, use a wire trace of at least 2 ft. in length. Once you have seen the teeth of a big pike, you'll understand why! The use of swivels is even more important in spinning than any other method, and to keep them in top form, a dab of light oil, applied with a soft brush, will keep them revolving freely and free from rust. Most spinning lures, including plugs, provide plenty of weight for casting, but in certain conditions, extra lead might be required. When selecting spinning leads, always get the anti-kink types, as spinning with ordinary weights will soon put a nasty kink in your line, causing untold 'birds nests' and tangles in the reel and rod-rings. Anti-kink 'vanes' are useful equipment for the spinning man, as they have the effect of reversing any line-twist that occurs during fishing.

As for the lures themselves, there's an even larger selection than floats, so choose wisely. Purely spinning lures include revolving or wobbling spoons and Devon minnows, which are all designed to imitate the action of a small wounded fish. They come in many sizes and colours and include spinning 'flights', to which small dead fish can be attached. Plugs do not spin, but are made to wriggle or dive, and here again, the choice is a wide one. Making your own lures can be a very worthwhile occupation and could also save the beginner a lot of money.

Of the available lures, I've had good results with the 'Mepps' range of spoons, 'Voblex' lures, which have a rubber, fish-like body; and a particular surface-fishing plug that's shaped and coloured like a miniature banana. Most of these lures are liberally armed with hooks, so keep them in a handy plastic container out of harm's way; the special tackle boxes with several cantilever trays are also good for this purpose.

For landing small to medium pike, an ordinary landing net can be used, but for anything larger, I wouldn't recommend it. A pike's teeth can make short work of nets, so when your fish is ready to come ashore, use a 'gaff'. This is a large, sharp hook attached to a handle, and, in my view, is often badly misused. The correct way to gaff a pike is to draw the point under its chin – or smooth membrane beneath the lower jaw. He can then be lifted out by the jawbone and will suffer very little damage as a result. Pike can also be landed by 'beaching' on certain occasions, but the fish must be thoroughly beaten before being slid up the bank, and the tackle must be sturdy enough for the purpose.

To cast a spinning lure from a fixed spool reel, the lure should be reeled up to within 12 in. of the rod-top. The pick-up on the reel will be opened, with the forefinger trapping the line against the spool. The cast is made by holding the rod to one side, parallel with the bank, at an angle of roughly 30° to the vertical. The rod is then swung gently backwards behind the shoulder and brought forward and across in a steady swing over the water, with the cast finishing when the rod is at right angles to the bank. Just before the end of the cast, a slight 'flick' should be imparted to increase the speed of the lure, at the same time, the forefinger must be released from the spool. Constant practice will improve your casting, and after a while, you'll be able to make quite long casts, without splashing the lure on the surface of the water. For fishing deep, the lure will be allowed to sink almost to the bottom before the reel pick-up is engaged, and line reeled in to commence the spin. Generally, this should be done in short 'spurts', allowing the bait to sink occasionally, to imitate a wounded fish.

For shallow and mid-water spinning, the lure is reeled in almost immediately it hits the water. As a general rule, spin fast and shallow for smaller pike, and deep and slow for larger fish. Plugs will almost always be fished on or near the surface, and for best results, vary the speed and action with every few feet of retrieve.

Some difficulty might be experienced when removing treble hooks from pike, and for this purpose, a 'gag' should be employed. The gag has a powerful spring action which is closed, when not in use, by a metal holding clip. When opened in the pike's mouth, it holds the jaws apart for easier removal of the hooks; which will usually be carried out with pliers or forceps. Be careful! Make sure the gag is properly secured before you start – and *never*, ever put your fingers in the mouth of a large pike unless the gag is in place. Those wicked teeth, which actually point backwards, are designed to hold the pike's prey securely in place ready for a one-way trip – down the throat! Most gags are made with savage points on each arm, so please cover these with rubber tubing to prevent damage to the pike's jaw.

The question of keepnets for pike doesn't arise, as they are nearly always returned to the water after capture. If pike must be killed however, owing to a special club rule, or if a fish is required for a glass case, then he should be hit over the back of the head with something smooth and heavy. It's such a long time since I killed a pike, I must admit that the idea has little appeal for me.

For keeping livebait fresh, an ordinary keepnet can be used, but where the angler is roving around the water, searching all the likely spots, a special bait kettle is available. Where livebaits are not needed for more than a couple of hours, an ordinary plastic bucket will do, but however your small fish are kept, always protect them from direct sunlight.

In conclusion, always observe the 'closed' season rules when fishing for pike on club or restricted waters. Many of these forbid piking before October, and although summer pike fishing seems to be gaining in popularity, I usually reserve my pike expeditions to autumn and winter, when spinning and bait-fishing takes on an atmosphere all of its own. In any case, I'm likely to be fully occupied with carp and tench in the summer months and this season, in most years, is all too short.

CHAPTER 9

Barbel

I warn you, if you take up serious barbel fishing, *you're* the one likely to be hooked! I know of nothing quite like the sinewy, dogged fight of a good barbel, small wonder it's a fish that is almost worshipped by dedicated anglers who think nothing of spending countless hours in search of just one good fish.

Hook a barbel of about 2 lb. and your fine tackle will be well tested; fish over four pounds will need all the skill of the novice angler to land, and if you're lucky enough to get a six or seven pounder, you'll need strong equipment – and a strong rod arm as well! Barbel over 13 lb. have been caught, but I'd advise you to avoid the really big fellows until you are properly equipped and experienced to deal with them.

Unlike the majority of coarse fish, the barbel is found in relatively few places and those are all rivers. He's essentially a fish of the fast, clear water and long gravelly runs. The two main English barbel rivers are the Thames and Hampshire Avon, but in more recent years he's found his way into other waters like the Dorset Stour, the Trent, Yorkshire Swale and Derwent. King's Weir on the river Lea near Cheshunt is quite a good all-round barbel fishery for small- to medium-sized fish, and there are some very good ones in the river Kennet in Berkshire.

On the Thames, where the water is often thick and coloured, the barbel are sometimes difficult to locate, but in the clear rivers (and don't ignore side-streams) they may often be seen lying still or 'turning over' on the gravel bottom. In years past, huge catches of these fish were made at places like Shepperton on Thames, Sunbury and Hampton Court; even the little river Wey near Godalming and Guildford produced good barbel. However, the modern angler's best chance would be the Royalty Fishery at Christchurch, the Throop stretch of the Dorset Stour, or the middle reaches of the Trent.

Baits: it is always difficult to generalise on baits, but in order of my own success I would suggest lobworm, luncheon meat, breadpaste and big bunches of maggots. Different baits work well on different waters, and in some parts of the country a good strong cheese paste will take fish when nothing else will. Some experiments are now being carried out using small livebaits (or deadbaits) like minnows and tiny gudgeon, but although I've given these a good try, I've had no success. Still, like chub, barbel will eat almost anything, so some experimenting with exotic or unusual baits will always be worthwhile.

When groundbaiting for barbel, use smaller scraps of the hookbait – and nothing else, where fish are very shy and can be seen lying in the swim. For deep, fast water, and particularly when fishing at long range, a heavier groundbait can be used.

Tackle: when it comes to tackle, I suggest you take a look at a good illustration of a big barbel or better still, study one at close range in an aquarium. Those muscular flanks, strong spoon-shaped fins, powerful tail and slim, torpedo shape are designed for one thing – strength. So remember that when selecting your barbel tackle.

I don't know any rivers where *only* small barbel exist, so I can't seriously recommend roach tackle for catching the smaller fish. Since most barbel inhabit the fast runs and deep pools of the river, the two main fishing methods are trotting the stream and legering. For the first method, using float tackle, the trotting rod, fixed spool reel and cork-bodied float, as used for chub, will be ideal. The 'Aerial' centrepin reel can also be used – if you have one. For legering at fairly long range, particularly in deep, fast water, nothing less powerful than the carp rod should be considered.

Barbel are one of the most powerful of all the freshwater fish, so lines should be strong. For trotting, use from 4 lb. to 6 lb., but go a little heavier for legering, say from 6 lb. to 10 lb. Carefully chosen forged hooks are a must, and they should be needle-sharp; the barbel has a tough, rubbery mouth like a carp.

Particular attention should be paid to knots which, on most tackles, are the weakest point. These should be tied with extra care and strength, for you could owe the catch of a lifetime to this detail! The size of your hook will depend on the bait being used and, for a large bunch of maggots (which takes good barbel in many waters), a size 12 would be just suitable, but for larger baits – like big balls of breadpaste and luncheon meat, or bunches of lobworms, chunks of sausage, etc. – use hooks within the 8 to 2 range, according to the shyness of the fish. Too large a hook and bait can scare the fish off.

Never keep barbel in keepnets, they will not take well to captivity and have a particularly vicious dorsal fin which can make short work of an expensive net. Landing nets, too, should be as large as possible, for although the barbel is not a deep-bodied fish, he is unusually long, from snout to tail, for his weight. Consequently, a net with long, wide arms will be required.

Methods: one of the most pleasant ways I know of catching barbel is trotting the stream, with float tackle. On the middle reaches of the Hampshire Avon, for example, this is sometimes done from a boat moored across the stream, trotting fairly heavy float tackle down between the weed-beds. On the whole, barbel are shy fish, so float fishing is mostly carried out at long range, and 'trots' of up to fifty yards are not uncommon. Groundbaiting for this method is important, and in fast water needs to be weighted with stones. Any good solid bread-and-meal mix will do, using the minimum of water, enclosing the groundbait around the stones, and including some of the hook-bait. These groundbait balls should be about the size of a cricket ball and dropped just over the downstream side of the boat. In the strong current they provide an attractive and consistent trickle of food right down to where your bait should be lying. 'Holding back' the float at the end of a swim down often produces a fish, but if chub are around, you might be bothered by them. But, in the main, your barbel will be taken on the bottom.

Legering in fast water will need fairly heavy leads to hold the bait in position, and the best weight for this is the Arlesey bomb, anything from $\frac{1}{4}$ oz. to 1 oz. in weight, according to the speed and power of the water. A good average length of 'trail' (the line between weight and hook) would be 12 in. In weirpools and shallow rivers and streams, the 'rolling leger' can be used to good effect; simply use a leger weight light enough to roll along the bed of the stream with the current, following it through to the end of the pool or swim. Bite detection will vary with these two different legering methods. With the 'static' bottom leger, the rod can be placed in a rest pointing up at an angle of 45°, and bites will usually register as 'thumps' on the rod-top. With barbel, these can be quite sudden and pronounced, although on some waters, a steady 'pull' is experienced when the fish moves off with the bait, pulling the rod around in no uncertain fashion. Be ready for these bites, otherwise your rod and tackle could finish up in the river!

When fishing the rolling leger, the angler should be standing holding the rod. As the bait and weight 'bumps' along the bottom, travelling the stream in search of fish, bites will actually be felt as a pull or knock (or both) on the rod and line. These bites, whether on static or rolling leger, should always be struck at once. Groundbaiting for both these methods can be useful, but use groundbait sparingly, and restrict it to samples of the hook bait.

Striking a barbel should consist of a steady, half-upwards-half-sideways sweep of the rod, in the opposite direction to which the 'pull' has been made. Once you've hooked your fish, be prepared for a battle royal, if he's a big one; for his first unstoppable runs will give you quite a surprise – and not a few anxious moments. After a few minutes, he'll still appear as strong and determined as when you first hit him, and you'll begin to wonder who's really winning! Steady, firm pressure will tell however, but be sure to steer his head away from any obvious snags like weedbeds, mooring buoys, poles, etc.

Many a good barbel has been lost 'at the net', so keep cool, make sure that he's tired out, and handle the net *very* carefully. Personally, I consider netting a barbel to be a two-man job, and I advise you to think the same way. The barbel's fight at the end of a line is usually so determined, he'll virtually fight himself to a standstill, after a while. So when you finally return him to the water (which you will, I'm sure, as soon as possible) hold him firmly in the river with his head facing upstream until he regains some strength. Never face him downstream, as he could drown. This recovery could take quite a few minutes, and I can remember Alan Vare holding an exhausted 9 lb. barbel in this way for at least 25 minutes.

CHAPTER 10

Dace and Bleak

Almost essentially fish of the river and stream, dace and bleak will often be found sharing the same water, invariably in the company of roach. Of the two, dace will reach a much larger size, although one over a pound should be looked upon as a specimen. A dace of 1½ lb. would be approaching the record, and you're much more likely to catch them at an average size of about 3 oz. to 6 oz. Bleak can be caught from about 1 in. to 3 in. long, and if you should ever get one over 5 oz., put it in a glass case. Using a single maggot on a tiny hook, bleak can be taken in large numbers, and where it is allowed, competition anglers go for lots of bleak to swell their match weights.

I can say little more about these two fish, except to mention that some good dace can be caught in the Thames, Hampshire Avon and its tributaries, the Kennet, Lea, Great Ouse and many river systems in the north of England. They are also present in some of the Scottish game waters, where they occasionally fall to a trout fisherman's artificial fly.

Baits: the best all-round bait for both dace and bleak is the maggot, and although my own largest dace were all caught on the tail of a lobworm, fished at the tail of a weirpool, I can claim little credit for them as I was, to be honest, after big chub at the time!

In the heat of summer, these two fish can also be tempted with tiny pieces of breadcrust, fished very close to the surface, and I must confess that this is my favourite method. Dace will often be taken on the dry fly but, as you know, I'm avoiding this type of fishing here, as it's much too complex for the novice coarse fisherman.

Tackle: your roach tackle will be ideal for these two fish, but hook sizes and line strength should both be finer. If you fish specifically for bleak, however, then a hook as small as size 20 would be an asset. Some dace and bleak fishermen will often reduce their line strength to ½ lb. or ¾ lb. for small bleak and larger, shy dace, but such fragile line needs very careful handling and I would advise you to avoid them, at least until you've gained some more experience.

Bleak and smaller dace can usually be landed without the aid of a landing net, but it is as well to carry one with you; you might run into a good roach or something even heavier, when bleaking. If you fish a competition and decide to go for bleak, you'll need a keepnet to retain them for weighing-in, and a special net with 'minnow' size mesh will be necessary.

Methods: at the risk of causing some bad feeling, I must confess that I am not a very keen 'match' fisherman. No, when the competition boys are filling their nets with tiny fish, I'm usually to be found tucked away behind the reeds, a long way from the match, 'doing my own thing', as it were. If it's a good dace water, I know I won't get the larger ones among all the noise and commotion of a match, as dace are really quite shy when they get over the pound size, so I go where it's quiet and, using very light float tackle, I trot the stream with a couple of maggots or a very small piece of breadcrust on the hook, tossing an occasional handful of cloud groundbait or a few bits of soaked bread well upstream of my swim, from time to time, particularly if the water is running at a fair rate.

With this method, the bait should be presented reasonably high in the water. But, if bites are few and far between, try altering the bait depth until it's just tripping the bottom. If the bait is small enough (and remember this means the use of a tiny hook) you will probably run into bleak as well, and if they are about, a roach or bream as well. Another of my little warnings here; dace waters often hold big chub and on the big rivers, these could run over four pounds apiece, so remember, if you hook one of these on a 20 hook to $\frac{3}{4}$ lb. line, it will be a miracle if you get it on the bank!

CHAPTER II

Miscellaneous Species

One of the interests and delights of coarse fishing is the wide variety of different fish that can be found in our still and flowing waters. Quite often, these 'surprises' are caught by anglers fishing for the more common species like roach, bream, pike or tench, but even if the catch is a disappointing one, it will pay you to pause, study the fish in question, and spare a moment to wonder at the almost never-ending delights of nature. A description of the various fish that you might encounter follows.

Gudgeon: this bottom-feeding fish is not unlike a small barbel, but can be identified by his two mouth 'barbules' or whiskers, whereas the barbel has four. He loves fast, gravelly runs in rivers and streams, but will occasionally be found in clean, still waters. The gudgeon is often regarded as a nuisance when he takes a bait meant for larger fish, as he will register quite a strong bite on float or leger tackles. He rarely reaches a weight exceeding $3\frac{1}{2}$ oz.

Common Eel: this snake-like fish lives in freshwater rivers, lakes and ponds, travelling to mid-Atlantic to breed. The young eels return to the river estuaries as elvers – in huge numbers, travelling right through the river systems, and sometimes moving overland to seek out suitable waters. The general colouring varies between greyish-silver to greenish-brown, according to age. The largest recorded rod-caught British eel weighed 8 lb. 10 oz. Some anglers make a study of the larger specimens, and many big eels are captured every season. Any eel over 2 lb. fights well at the end of a line, but stout hooks and tackle are required, even a wire trace, as the eel's teeth are numerous and sharp. Good eel baits are large worms or small dead fish, whole or cut into pieces, fished on the bottom. Fish at night for best results.

Flounder: a small flatfish which is related to the saltwater plaice and dab, the flounder will travel quite long distances into freshwater. The body colour is greeny-brown, with a white underside and orange-spotted fins. They will reach a weight of over 5 lb., but the average size is considerably smaller. Strictly a bottom-feeding fish, the flounder can be caught with earthworms, maggots or small pieces of lugworm or ragworm.

Zander (Pike-Perch): originally introduced from Europe, this half-perch, half-pike species is now established in a few British waters, notably the Great Ouse Relief Channel in Norfolk and the Duke of Bedford's ponds at Woburn Abbey. The zander is a voracious feeder and can be caught on worms and livebaits. Specimens over 10 lb. have been caught in Norfolk, but they grow to a much larger size on the Continent.

Catfish (Wels): a native of the river Danube and other eastern European waters, the Wels can now be found in several localised fisheries, including the lakes at Claydon Park, Bedfordshire, the Duke of Bedfordshire's Woburn ponds, and parts of the Great Ouse river system nearby. Strictly a bottom-feeding 'scavenger', the catfish will take a variety of baits; large bunches of lobworms, dead or live, fish, etc. The British rod-caught record is a fish of 33 lb. 12 oz. from Claydon. The larger catfish is a strong, dogged fighter, and stout tackle will be required. In colour, he is a muddy olive-green, with mottled flanks; he has a wide, large mouth and six 'whiskers' or barbules; two very long ones on the nose and four shorter ones on the lower jaw.

Grey Mullet: essentially a sea fish, but will move into freshwater estuaries during the summer, returning to the sea in the autumn. This is a handsome fish with 'metallic' blue-green colouring and pale brown belly; he fights well when hooked but is difficult to catch, being strictly a vegetarian feeder. There are three separate species: thick-lipped, thin-lipped and golden, which are difficult to tell apart. The record rod-caught thick-lipped grey mullet stands at just over 10 lb. Strong roach tackle is advised, with small baits like a single maggot, balls of breadpaste, etc., on a small hook.

The following fish will be found in many waters all over Britain and for the purposes of coarse fishing, can be disregarded as sporting fish. They will probably be better remembered by the 'bent pin and jam jar' brigade, who, after serving an apprenticeship with these little tiddlers during an hour's fishing after school, were probably attracted to the pursuit of much bigger game.

Minnow: usually to be found in clear, unpolluted rivers and streams. Has light cream-coloured fins, silvery belly and pale green mottled and striped sides. Very often present in large shoals, and will reach a maximum length of 4 in., although the average will be nearer to $1\frac{1}{2}$ in. A good livebait for perch, the minnow can be caught using lightest roach tackle, with a tiny float and a $\frac{1}{2}$ in. length of thin worm on the smallest hook you can find. Can also be captured in the special 'minnow traps' available in tackle shops.

Ruffe: sometimes called the pope, this spiny, bottom-feeding fish loves deep, slowly flowing rivers and side-streams, and will rarely be seen until he takes an angler's bait – that is being fished for something larger! An unusual feature ·is the two dorsal fins, the first with sharp spines, the second more rounded and mottled. The ruffe has an off-white belly, greeny-brown sides and a speckled tail. He will take worm and maggot baits, and reaches a maximum weight of about 4 oz.

Bullhead: often known as the 'miller's thumb', he prefers shallow, stony areas of brooks, streams and clear lakes. The head is large and rounded, while the body is a mottled olive-brown. There are two spiny dorsal fins. Rarely exceeds 4 in. in length. Best bait: worm.

Stickleback: the two separate species of stickleback are the three-spined and ten-spined. When spawning, the male three-spined fish has a bright red colouring to the belly and sides, while the male ten-spined has a black belly and throat. These fish seldom exceed 4 in. in length and are found in many waters, from fast-running streams to clear ponds and lakes. Can be taken on the tackle and bait described for minnows.

Loach: there are two loaches, the stone loach and spined loach, both liking the stony parts of clear streams and rivers, and sometimes lakes, where the water is pure. The spined loach is the smaller of the two, and both fish have minute scales and speckled fins and tails. Maximum length: (stone) $7\frac{1}{2}$ in.; (spined) $5\frac{1}{4}$ in.

CHAPTER 12

Hints and Tips

The following notes are the result of many months of sporadic 'memo' writing; on the backs of wrappers and tickets, menus, packets – anything that came to hand at the time. Added to the details from already published articles and diary entries, they form a somewhat haphazard but, we hope, valuable supplement to the various sections in this book devoted to separate species of fish.

Care of tackle: rods should never be left in wet rod-bags. After fishing, take the rod from its bag, wipe down with a soft dry cloth and replace in a *dry* bag. Most rod-bags have a tape loop for hanging, and your rods are best stored by hanging on a wall, vertically, in a cool, dry place – not a garage or cellar.

To prevent line sticking to your rod in misty or damp weather, coat the rod lightly beforehand with silicone furniture polish. A broken rod top-joint can be repaired, in an emergency, with strong cellotape or insulating tape. Get the broken top to your tackle dealer as soon as possible for a professional repairing job.

Rod ferrules should be cleaned and lightly greased (outside) after fishing trips. The interiors of female ferrules can be treated with beeswax or graphite. Rod holdalls tend to get soaked at the bottom; dry these out completely after each fishing trip.

Always dry reels thoroughly after use, and oil (with light machine oil) before each outing. Keep all your loose hooks dry and separated by attaching the points to foam rubber or dry felt pads during transit. This will prevent them from rubbing together and causing the points to become blunted. Nylon line should be kept in the dark, in a dry container. Wash dirty keep-nets and landing-nets with an occasional swish in a light detergent solution. Store them in a dry place, away from mice – who love a smelly net, especially an oil-dressed cotton one.

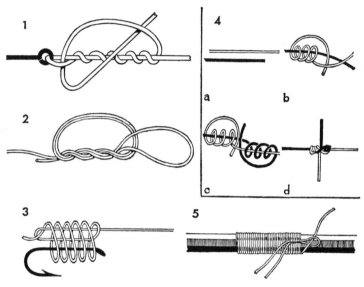

Fisherman's knots. (1) Half blood knot for joining line to an eyed hook, spinner, swivel, etc. (2) Overhand knot for making a loop in line. (3) Knot for tying a spade-end hook. (4) Knot for joining two pieces of line. (5) Whipping for rods, floats, etc. To complete, pull the line through by means of loop, then carefully trim off the ends.

Don't leave damp socks inside wellingtons and waders; they could rot the linings. Always dry out waders and gumboots thoroughly after use – but don't use excessive heat, it could ruin the rubber. Umbrellas must always be dried after use to prevent the ribs rusting and the cover rotting. Open the wet brolley and leave over the bath for about two hours, to dry thoroughly.

Stuck rod ferrules: two pieces of rubber inner tube, each

2 in. × 12 in. will help; wrap one piece clockwise around the first joint, the other piece anti-clockwise around the second, applying the rubber under some tension. This will give two firm, easily held grips to unstick the ferrules with a firm twisting motion.

Removing a hook from cloth: hold the shank of the hook firmly and scrape the cloth down the outside of the hook towards the point; this should free the point, enabling the barb to be lifted free. The best tool for scraping is the back of a knife blade or a thumb nail.

Releasing undersized fish: a very small fish can be quickly unhooked, without handling, by sliding your forefinger and thumb down the line, grasping the shank of the hook and gently shaking it just over the water.

Hooking lively worms: lobworms sometimes wriggle so much in the hand, that they are difficult to hook. A sharp tap between the fingers (not too hard) will stun the worm sufficiently to allow easy hooking.

Maggots: can be kept for long periods in a domestic 'fridge – but avoid bad feeling by making sure the lady of the house will allow it!

Worms: are best stored in a dark, cool place – not the 'fridge! A cellar, coal-shed or brick-built garage is ideal.

Tench rake: a bottom rake for tench swims can be made by joining two ordinary garden rake heads 'back to back with the prongs facing outwards. Tie together firmly with strong plastic-coated wire or nylon rope. Through the eyes on the rake-heads, attach a 30 ft. length of strong nylon rope with a wrist-loop at the other end. The rake should be cast out, allowed to sink, then pulled slowly through the swim, avoiding thick water-lily roots and fallen trees, etc. All resulting rubbish should be stacked well away from the waterside and preferably hidden under bushes, etc.

Spare tackle: always keep a spare reel, spool of line, floats, hooks, weights, etc., in your tackle bag – don't be caught out 30 miles from home!

Club cards, river licences, permits, etc.: keep these *in* your bag or tackle box, preferably in a waterproof bag or wallet.

Hooks: always carry a small sharpening stone for hooks. Even new hooks are not always sharp enough. To remove a hook from a leathery-mouthed fish like a carp, if it is well embedded, cut off the line near the hook, and pass the hook *out* through the lip of the fish. To make a 'barbless' hook for fishing for bleak and other very small fish, simply snip off the barb with small pliers. Don't stick hooks into hats, coat lapels, etc., material retains moisture and perspiration and can cause hooks to rust.

Tares: are proving to be a killing bait for roach. These dark brown, pea-like seeds are about the size of an elderberry and should be boiled and simmered, like hempseed, until they are soft and have turned a purple colour. Try boiling them with hempseed, for added attraction. Wheat grains, tares and hemp can also be 'cooked' by putting them in a vacuum flask or jar, adding boiling water and screwing down the top. They should be ready when you reach the waterside. Hemp can be made more attractive by adding a little soda to the water; this turns the grains a nice dark shade, almost black.

Weighing: when weighing large fish, always use a nylon net, plastic bag or other soft container; *never* stick the hook of a spring balance through the gills or mouth of a fish.

Times for fishing: for most coarse fish, the best times for fishing are early and late in summertime, from 4 a.m. to 10 a.m. and 6 p.m. to dark. If you get up very early to go fishing, and fish right through the day, make up your sleep somehow; fishing in very warm weather can be very tiring. Try a nap in the afternoon – if the fish aren't biting.

Keeping an album: a fishing album or diary is also a good idea. The details, pictures and information about catches on different waters can be extremely valuable for future trips; and they'll also make interesting fireside reading at a later date.

Groundbait: when fishing for rudd in lakes and ponds, make a groundbait by lightly baking some white breadcrust in the oven. This should be cut into small pieces and tied to lengths of fine nylon or cotton, the loose end being attached to a small stone or pebble. Cast out to the fringes of lily pads, etc., to attract the rudd to your own bait. To get dace and bleak feeding merrily, try 'caster' maggots. When casting a bait to a visible chub in clear water, try casting behind the fish; he'll often turn quickly and grab the bait. When deadbait legering for pike, groundbait with handfuls of chopped small, silvery fish.

Spinning: when spinning for perch and pike, try speeding up the rate of retrieve right at the end of the cast. These fish often follow a lure right into the bank, and a sudden spurt to the spinner could induce the fish to take.

Bream: if you've got a good shoal of bream on the feed, always return each one you catch *away* from your swim. Muddy clouds in the water can indicate a shoal of bream on the feed – walk down the river until you find one.

Don't get hurt: if you catch a perch or ruffe, look out for the spines on the dorsal fins and gill-covers; they can really hurt! The barbel also has a vicious spine on his dorsal fin; take care when handling – and watch your keepnet, this spine can create havoc. When removing a hook from a big chub, watch out for his throat teeth – they can damage your fingers.

Lines: always cut at least 3 ft. of line from the reel before or after each fishing trip; line frays or gets weak at the 'business' end. If line becomes badly coiled or kinked, give it a good firm pull, over about 2 rod lengths; this should straighten it for a time. To keep nylon line floating, use a good silicone 'Mucilin'; to sink a line, rub with fine mud or a weak solution of detergent and water. To make a small coil of lead wire for hemp fishing, or fishing a slowly sinking bait, wind a short length of fine lead wire tightly around a needle. Flatten the ends to grip the line.

Floats: when float fishing in heavy water, use two float caps, in case one breaks. When fishing from a boat, small items of tackle, penknives, lighters, etc., can be attached to small cork blocks; if they fall overboard, they float and can be easily retrieved.

Clothing: in wet weather, use a small hand towel as a scarf, to prevent water running down your neck. Wear heavy old socks over wellington boots when walking on slippery surfaces like wet concrete, rock, timber, etc. In very cold, wet weather, always wear an outer 'layer' of waterproof material; even a thin plastic mac gives good insulation. In such weather, cover baits and tackle with a waterproof groundsheet to stop them getting sodden. Always wear dull clothing as a 'camouflage' when fishing; bright white shirts and gaudy coats are easily seen by fish. *Don't scare the fish:* don't stamp or run around on the riverbank; fish easily sense vibrations; treat fish in the same way you would a field of shy rabbits.

Be tidy: take all empty packets, polythene bags, sweet wrappers and discarded nylon line, etc., away with you when you leave the waterside – and make sure all your friends do the same.

CHAPTER 13

The Country Code, Safety and the Law

Always lock gates after you, if you don't, cattle could stray into growing crops, become bogged down in mud or damaged by road vehicles. Don't light fires in dry weather and don't throw discarded matches into dry vegetation – even if you think they're not alight.

Don't leave litter around the fishery; loose nylon can trap and kill wild birds and small mammals. Glass objects like bottles can cause fires by concentrating hot sun on one spot, or if broken, can damage the feet of cattle. Plastic bags and cups, ring-pulls from tins and other plastic objects are unsightly and do not rot; take them home with you for disposal, or use any litter bins provided.

Respect trees, shrubs, flowers and other wild plants. Don't disturb or hurt water fowl and other wild birds – they have more natural right to the countryside than you. Don't disturb farm animals like calving cows and laying hens. Don't disturb bird's nests or take eggs. Don't tread on growing crops, keep well to the public footpaths or edges of fields. Don't park cars or motorcycles where they might obstruct farmers' or other people's working or private vehicles. Keep quiet when fishing; transistor radios and loud conversation can annoy other people. Don't shout to someone on the other side of a lake or river; sound carries quickly across water. Be extra quiet after dark; farm folk rise early and go to bed early. Always produce your fishing permit or fishing licence when asked by someone in authority. Don't fish too close to other anglers, and never leave your rod unattended for long periods; someone else might want to fish that swim.

Always oblige a fellow angler urgently needing a spare hook or some bait. Always help younger anglers. If you're planning a fishing trip and you have a car, take an old-age pensioner with you – it could be the highlight of his year. Don't over-groundbait a water, it can go sour on the bottom with adverse results for the fish. Always clean up your swim when you leave; make it look as though nobody has ever been there.

Water pollution: always watch for signs of dead, diseased or distressed fish. Any cases should be reported to the appropriate river authority, angling club official or local police as soon as possible. Should you observe crop-spraying activity near any fishery, whether by aircraft or other means, report it, as above.

The law: you can't fish *anywhere* in the country, and even if you have a fishing club ticket or permission from the owner to fish a private water, you might still need a river board licence, so check this before travelling long distances to fish. Juniors under 12, or in some cases 16, are not allowed on some fisheries; check this before fishing. Watch the coarse fishing close season (the time when fishing is discontinued to allow fish to spawn without interruption); this varies in different areas; get the facts. Watch out for waters that are closed each year for duck shooting or other reasons. One rod only is allowed on many waters, so don't fish with two baited rods unless this rule has been checked. Never take live or dead coarse fish away from any water, it is an offence on most fisheries.

Observe 'single bank' fishing rules and never cross strictly private property to get to your swim. The parking of cars and other vehicles is not allowed on or near many waters – don't break the rules. Never fish at night if there is a no night-fishing rule, and don't set night-lines for fish like eels, etc., this is not allowed on most inland waters.

And note the following general points:

Hooks: they can be very dangerous – take care, keep them away from children and animals. If a hook becomes embedded to the barb in your flesh, don't try your own surgical skills, get to a doctor or hospital right away.

Weirpools: are dangerous! Always wear good gripping shoes or boots when fishing near them. Watch out for slippery banks, platforms and 'sills'.

Swimming: is a 'must' for anglers, young or old. You're going to spend a lot of leisure time by the waterside, so if you can't swim, take lessons right away; it could save your life. Better still, take life-saving instruction – you could save someone else's life.

Boats: can be dangerous. *Never* stand up in a boat, and never take a boat out in rough weather, even if it's only threatening; even some medium-sized lakes are subject to sudden squalls. Always 'drive' on the correct side of the river and always give way to sail-boats if you have power. Always tie up a boat securely and allow for any tide when deciding the length of the painter. Watch out for weirpools, crosscurrents and rocks or shoals.

Lightning: it can strike twice in the same place! *Never* fish under trees when lightning is about.

Banks: can be insecure because of land subsidence, mud, steep slopes, floodwater, etc. Make sure your bank is firm before starting to fish.

Mud: can be treacherous; watch out for sinking sand or quicksands. Avoid short-cuts across marshy ground, unless you know every inch of the territory well.

Bulls: these animals are dangerous! They can seriously injure, even kill. Watch out for them, particularly in meadows where they can creep up on you quietly. Make sure you have a fast exit like a gate, stile or tall tree. As a last resort, face the bull, raise both arms and shout very loudly.

Bites and stings: can be nasty, particularly if you have a sensitive skin. Always carry emergency treatment like 'Waspeeze' or a small bottle of vinegar. Always use a good insect-repellent when fishing in the summer and autumn. To avoid snakebite, always wear gumboots, waders or hard leather calf-length boots. *Parking cars:* always park on firm ground, with the handbrake on and the engine in gear. Don't park on a steep slope near the water; heavy rain could cause subsidence under the wheels. Never keep pets and other animals in parked cars, in hot weather, with the windows closed; they could easily suffocate. *Casting:* don't endanger others with flying hooks, spinners, leads, etc. Watch out for passing boats before casting.

CHAPTER 14

A Day's Fishing with Arthur and Alan

Although young Philip has only recently taken up coarse fishing, he already has some good roach to his credit, so Alan and I decided to take him for a day's fishing on a good 'mixed' fishery . . .

'Right, here we are lads, the dawn's just breaking through the trees, the lake's as still as a millpond and there's just a nice touch of mist on the water. I've an idea the tench will be feeding this morning; worth getting up early for, eh Phil?

'Set the gear down here, we groundbaited this swim – and another one round the corner – last night, so I'll just throw in a little more groundbait while you and Alan make up the tackle. Here, quietly now, look at that, just out from the edge of those reeds. They're needle bubbles, and that means tench lads – they're here already!

'What's that Alan? You're going to the other swim? Right, good luck to you, we'll make a start here. That's good Phil, your float's cocked nicely. What bait are you using? Three maggots on a number 12 hook? Good. I put plenty of maggots in the groundbait.

'Now, I'll just cast about six yards to your left, but I'll try a piece of white breadflake, then if you stick to maggots, we'll see which bait the tench are taking. Pssst! Phil, look – about ten yards to your right – more needle bubbles, watch out – and watch your float carefully, the tench should be at your bait very soon. Crikey! They're all around your float now – look

118

at it wobble, must be two or three feeding on the groundbait. Now, take hold of the rod-handle, steady, don't move the line . . . now! there it goes! Your float's away, running and submerging at the same time . . . now, strike! Good, he's on! It's a nice one too, look at that rod bend. Watch him Phil, he's making a dash for those lily pads – good man, that's right, give him some sidestrain.

'Now he's tiring, well done Phil, just steer him over the submerged landing net . . . got him! There, your very first tench; let's weigh him in the bottom of the net. Three pounds four ounces – a beauty! No, let's not put him in a keepnet, it seems a shame; we'll just take a note of what we catch, then, if a specimen shows up, we'll take some pictures for the album.

'I wonder what Alan's doing, can't see him from here, perhaps he's busy catching tench. There! I'm into one now – it's not a bad one either; thanks, just sink the net down there. Good, now, steady, wait until he's played out, right, now I'll steer his head and shoulders over the rim of the net . . . now, lift the net - got him! He's only about two and a half pounds – not as big as yours, but he certainly fought well, the smaller ones often do.'

(Two hours later):
'Well Phil, the sun's well on the water now, the tench will probably go off the feed fairly soon, the bubbling seems to have stopped. How many did we get? Nine between us but nothing bigger than your three-and-a-quarter-pounder. Not a bad morning's sport – and did you notice how they ignored the maggots and came to the breadcrust about an hour ago? Let's get the tea flask out now, and go and see what Alan's been doing.

'Hello Al, you look pretty happy, what luck have you had? Sixteen crucian carp and two small tench, eh? Not bad, what did the largest crucian weigh? Pound and a half? That's quite a good 'un for this water. What's that Phil? You fancy a crucian or two? All right, drop in beside Alan. Scale your tackle down a bit, that's right, smaller float, smaller hook –

with one of those little marsh worms on. Fine, out she goes. Hold it, Alan's got another crucian; well done mate, it's about half a pound – and how they fight!

'Your float's moving Phil – now it's away; wait though, that's no crucian bite – ah, I thought so, bring him in, you've had those before, haven't you? Hold this damp cloth around him while you take the hook out; he's beautifully hooked right through the top lip – that's because you struck soon after the bite developed. If you'd let him go any longer, he might have taken the hook right back in the throat – and that would have made a nasty bit of surgery for the disgorger! Yes, watch out for that spiny dorsal fin of his, it can give you a nasty jab if you're not careful. Just look at his thick humped back and huge mouth! Great fish, perch – I really love 'em. Good, that's that, now let's put him back, over here in the next pool, well away from Alan's swim.

'Oh no! Alan's into another crucian. Notice how he uses the landing net Phil – even for the smaller ones.

'It's your turn now, put another worm on, good; it's going to be a lovely day, quite hot later on I shouldn't wonder. There, did you see your float just 'lift' out of the water about a quarter of an inch? That'll be a crucian. Wait now, your float's moving off, hold it . . . now! Strike! Marvellous, it's on! He's what? A real scrapper? You can say that again, these crucians just don't know when they're beaten. Look at him dart around the swim – he almost had Alan's tackle fouled up that time. Now you have him; that's it, slip the net under him . . . gently . . . good – got him!

'Hey, look there a moment – just to the left of Alan's float, by that bed of weed; I can see some needle bubbles – looks as though the tench are still about after all; that's probably because the sun hasn't quite reached this corner of the lake yet – the water's still shaded by those big elm trees on the island. You're going to do what Alan? Put on the tail of a big lobworm? Well, I hope it suits you! Yes, I know you mean on the hook – and you're probably right; remember how we took tench right through the daytime on lobworm bait last season?

'The bubbles are nearer your float now Alan, and wait – yes, there's a bite! Good man, he's on! Wow! That's some tench, look at the way he's churning up the mud; that's right, keep his head up, show him who's boss; no, he's not quite ready for netting yet – he's only making another dash for the lilies – now he's coming into the bank – he's definitely tiring – right, I'll take the net Alan; he's a good 'un all right, I just caught a glimpse of his side. O.K., slide him over the net . . . got him!

'There Phil, look at that for a beauty! Yes, he's over five pounds – five-two, actually, and they don't come a lot bigger than that on this water.

'How many crucians have you had now Phil? Six? That's quite good, but they seem to have gone off the feed now; in fact, it's all gone a bit quiet – too quiet. Aha! I thought so! Did you see those little fish scampering across the surface out there? There they go again – yes, I think it's a pike, see that big swirl, right by the lily pads? Too big for a perch; no wonder that shoal of crucians moved off. Let's have a council of war. All right Alan, that pike queered your swim, so you have first go at him. Watch this closely Phil, see how Alan has attached a twelve-inch wire trace to his line, with a small swivel at both ends. Now, see that? He's tied on a small 'Voblex' spinning lure. It has a moulded rubber head, a little spinning vane – and some treble hooks, of course. Now, watch how he flips the lure out with an easy swinging cast, just beyond the weed-bed. No, he's not letting it sink too deep, he knows the pike is feeding fairly close to the surface.

'Crikey! He's got it! No, it's not a big one, but it's putting up quite a scrap. See it trying to dash into the reeds? . . . Good, he's pretty well beaten now – you put the net under him, I hate gaffing pike. There he is. What a great little fish – all of six pounds I'd say – and beautifully marked.

'Well, I think we'd better give the water a rest now. What say we stretch our legs and walk right round the lake? We might spot a shoal of mirror carp over by the boathouse, and maybe that's where the tench have migrated to. Anyway, a good stiff walk won't hurt us after all that sitting about.'

(*About* 12.30 *p.m.*):
'Well men, I vote that a fair morning's sport. When the tench went off feed we all had plenty of crucian carp, plus some good plump rudd as a bonus. Now, I think it's time we thought about lunch; Alan's arranged it all with the lock-keeper across the way, his wife will make sure we get some piping hot bacon and eggs and a big pot of strong tea. After lunch, we're going to fish the river, starting with the weirpool. That's where the barbel should be, but don't get too excited Phil – they're not at all easy to catch!'

(*After an enjoyable lunch, we set up the tackle by the weirpool*):
'Now Phil, we'll show you how to fish for barbel. For this, we'll use the leger rod and step up the line strength to about six pounds. I always keep a spare spool of heavier line for my fixed spool reel so I can change over quickly. We won't use a float, the water's much too fast, so I'll run one of these Arlesey Bombs up the line, stopping it about two feet up with a small split-shot. Now I'll tie on a number six eyed hook – needle sharp, of course – now we're ready to start fishing. We'll use a big lobworm for bait, but I'll set the minnow trap as well, just under this big boulder. Dead minnows make quite a good bait for big barbel on this river.

'Yes, you take the tackle, I'll watch you. Good, a nice easy swing out. Try to bring the bait to rest right under the sill – the ledge – of the weir. I know it looks far too rough to hold fish, but believe me, that's where they are.

. 'No, don't put the rod down, keep hold of it, and feel the line between the reel and butt ring with your other hand. You'll feel a bite either as a sharp "pluck" on the line, or as a good steady pull on the top of the rod. If you feel a good pull, strike hard – the barbel's mouth is very tough and he'll put up quite a fight after he's hooked, particularly if he's a big one, so strike well to set the hook properly.

'I should watch your step around here, these rocks are very slippery. Never try to clamber over them – even to net a fish – there's about twelve feet of boiling, turbulent water down there and if you fell in, I doubt if anyone could help you. What's that? You felt a couple of plucks on the line? Good, that means fish, but it could be a gudgeon or ruffe. I should wait for a good steady pull.

'I see Alan's stationed himself at the tail of the pool, he loves that stretch, I think he's trotting the stream with float tackle, hoping for a chub or two. A grape-sized lump of bread-paste or cheese-paste makes a killing bait down there, or even a live minnow, floated down the side of the stream. We've both had some really good chub like that, but in the early season you'll find a few smaller barbel there as well.

'Whooosh! That was quite a professional barbel strike Phil – but you've missed him. He did what? Pulled your rod almost into the water? Yes, I know, I've had plenty of bites like that; never mind, try again.'

(*Two hours later*):
'Well Phil, I think we'll change our tactics – the barbel don't seem to be feeding under the sill. Let's move everything down a little, nearer to the centre of the pool. Yes, just about here, I've had some nice fish from this swim in the past. Keep your leger rig going, but put a swim-feeder on the line and fill it up with maggots; it will give a good weight for casting – and supply a regular trickle of groundbait just where you need it. You'll have to change your hook though, that lobworm hook's much too big. There, put this number ten spade-end hook on, with as many big maggots as it will hold. How many did you get on? Twelve? That's good, it's a choice-looking bunch all right. Now, out it all goes, right in the very centre of the weir-pool. Tighten up, good, now wait – and hold your rod, just like before.

'Bang! There's a good bite! Yes, it's hooked – but I don't think it's a barbel; no, I'm right, it's a roach – but it's a beauty! Must be a pound at least. Well done Phil, it's well hooked in the top lip. Put it back in the water. Good man . . . now, cast out again, same place as before.'

* * *

(*Later, at the lock-keeper's house*):

'Well chaps, let's call it a day; I'm sorry we couldn't fix you up with a barbel Phil, but perhaps they'll be feeding another time. Still, you can't grumble, you had four lovely roach from the pool – and finished up with a three-pound bream, and that's a good afternoon's work! Alan's four-pound chub from the stream was a lovely fish too, maybe we can all get down here again next week and do some really serious trotting. That's the beauty of a "mixed" fishery like this one; you have the best of both worlds – lake and river.

'Well, let's get back to the car. I don't know about you, but I'm feeling just a bit weary; won't have any trouble getting to sleep tonight!'

Index